Anonymous

Inflexible factors and other short pieces

Anonymous

Inflexible factors and other short pieces

ISBN/EAN: 9783337223885

Hergestellt in Europa, USA, Kanada, Australien, Japan

Cover: Foto ©Andreas Hilbeck / pixelio.de

Weitere Bücher finden Sie auf **www.hansebooks.com**

OTHER SHORT PIECES

BY

R. A. E., S. D. E., T. S. S., S. S. H., D. N. R.

AND OTHERS

NOT PUBLISHED

INFLEXIBLE FACTORS.

A collection of Frames for Verses and Essays, with other short Pieces, mostly lyrical in general character, arranged in Suites, Triptychs, Diptychs, Words for Illumination or to accompany Illustrations, Words for Music, and as Single Pieces, and frequently illustrating results from inflexible factors.

With a Prelude.

CONTENTS.

WORDS FOR ILLUMINATION OR TO
ACCOMPANY ILLUSTRATIONS:

Tower of Ivory!
The circling year.
The Song of the Rose.
A Climbing Rose.
With a jewelled "damoiselle."
An Iris.
A portrait.
A time serene.
Benedictus qui patitur.

WORDS FOR MUSIC.

FOUR SCHOOL AND COLLEGE SONGS:

Boating Song.
Far off friends.
The two Bobo'links.
Kineherd's song.

FOUR MINSTREL SONGS:

Molly True.
Elegy.
Mary far away.
Beyond the stars.

SERENADES AND MISCELLANEOUS SONGS:

My star.
Softly the night winds.
The stilly night.
Nearer, nearer.
In spring time.
Shamus Moriarty.
When the one I love is near me.
Shouldst thou stand on the golden stair.

FIVE DEVOTIONAL PIECES.

Cradle Song.
A Ranter's Hymn.

The adoration of the Magi.
Under the Crucifix.
At Whitsuntide.

SINGLE PIECES.

The Singer.
Terrible as an army with banners.
As I sailed.
Weighing.
When these winter nights are o'er.
Rest.
Despondency.
The Christian Church.
To Beneficence.
First of the train.
Sonnet.
Vestality.
The dreamers.
The Victims.
The Best Way, or My Way.
Hymn.
The Lost Lord.
Native Moments.
As years roll on.
Oh! time, oh! fate.
Where there is suffering.
Inflexible Factors.
O presence, unseen presence of the
one I love.
A Coming Change.
The grains of sand.
The Jesu-worshipper.
The Gamesters.
Aspiration.
As one led.

CONCLUDING NOTE.

APPENDIX.

A theory of the Origin (and transmission) of Organic Form.
A theory of Pattern (miscalled Design) in Nature.
A theory of the Origin of Rhythm.
The Sacerdote says.
Round on Round.
A Resumé of a System of Concentrated Residence.
Treatment of convicts (see the Dreamers).
A Method of quickly securing Accurate Proportion in Drawing from Objects (see the Story of a 12th Night Festival).

Postscripta: Backlook and Outlook. In the Laucustrine Abodes. The Democratic Idea. Of Binding and Binding. Etc., etc.
Note on the Independence of Motions.
Account of Patents.
The Origin of Xitria, etc.
Studies for a Preface to poems.
Letters relating to the hopeless vulgarity of the Human Race, etc.
Ahriman.

[See also Notes and prefaces to Xitria, and A 12th Night Festival, and Notebooks from cir. 1881.]

NOTE.

Some years ago I fell into the habit of hastily jotting down in pencil, fragments which I thought might be used in some connected or disconnected poetic form or forms. I thought of them as frames or scaffoldings for verses; and, for want of a better name, they are here called so. They are given as separate pieces, arranged in the groups, made up of these frames and more regular verses, to which, for any reason, they seemed most properly to belong. Most of them were written, each piece all at one time, and just as they stand here, except that they were written as prose. Some of them, however, were added to from time to time, or only completed long—perhaps years—afterward. The three forms of Love's chaplet show the only attempt made to carry the original notion into effect. For this attempt showed me that, however great the value of form, and whatever success attention to it might have with others, with me, in this case at least, the loss of spontaneity was not compensated for by the greater regularity of form. Later, becoming acquainted with the poems of Whitman and others, where the form has a value depending on something more subtle than a regularity which results merely from correspondence or approximate identity, rather than balance, of parts, I thought best to leave the pieces as they stood—pieces often commenced as frames for verses or essays, or as mere memoranda of a passing thought, yet sometimes ending as verses, though all written at a sitting—only they have been printed in lines which, it seemed, would make clearer, to the eye of a reader, the rhythms which, unperceived but not unfelt, fell spontaneous from the hand of the writer.

To these have been added, by permission, various pieces, by friends of the author and others, bearing on the themes coming under the several headings among which they are distributed. Most of their writers were, and are, unknown to each other. As several of them prefer to remain anonymous, the names of the authors of the poems are not given. And, instead, devices are used which will enable any of the authors who may later desire to claim their own, to do so, and without affecting the others.

Although, in a general way, anyone who perceives or reads of any form of suffering or happiness, however slight or remote it may be, will yet be likely, sooner or later, to look about, though only casually and vaguely, for some way of diminishing like sufferings or increasing like happinesses; and although, too, the gradual lessening of any

and all of the myriad forms of suffering or loss possible to sentient beings is the central impulse of evolution, yet these little pieces put forth no claim to assist in promoting changes, especially particular or definite changes. Alike, whether when telling of joy or sorrow, they are merely reflections, as from a mirror, consequent on chance perceivings of conditions which, almost in prevailing, imply, or seem likely in time to lead to, a change of form in the conditions which will succeed them.

But though no one particular change is aimed at, yet the general principle that where there is suffering, there there is a desirability of change, is certainly strongly felt, by one of their authors at least; and it is hoped will be felt by the reader, and the more felt, perhaps, after the reading of these little pieces. And, further, it is hoped reading them will help some to see more clearly how all hard-and-fast rules are bad masters; though rules are good servants, and even hard-and-fast rules, up to a certain point; if that point is one never to be reached, improvement, easing of the legally pinching shoe, the binding withe, the pressing weight, is never to be reached. If law is something received, external, and not evolved out of the divinity of man's highest aspirations after worthiness—worthiness of methods, of methods for securing the happiness of men and of their neighbors as themselves—then laws are hard-and-fast, and improvement of man's estate stops. But if rules are followed until a still more satisfactory rule is found and deliberately adopted by general consent, a constant improvement in man's estate must follow. Day before yesterday, by the waters of Babylon we sat down and wept; yesterday in Rama there was a voice heard, Rachel weeping for her children; last night the Waldenses and the Albigenses suffered, the fires of the Inquisition burned, the torture chambers of Nuremberg only showed what went on in every European town; toward morning the guillotine was erected; and so on; until to-day, at noon-day, American Indians cast a girl into the flames to protect them from a dire pestilence which has fallen on the tribe; the cannibalism, the eating of the little girl in Hayti goes on, to placate, by human sacrifice, the enemy of mankind—as with the Druids of old, as with the ancients of perhaps all peoples, Iphigenia's, Isaac's—Jesus dies upon the cross, " a full, perfect, and sufficient sacrifice " (horrible idea!), and the mass is celebrated, and the Anglican and American women go to the early celebration. In Russia, Catholics are harried by the government ecclesiastical system. And in China? In all dark coun-

tries? But for English interference, the modern spirit, improvement, the Suttee in India! How long, O Lord, how long will men prefer the flattery of their egotism in thinking that they hold the right—prefer it or some grosser gain—above every form of mercy?

> " Let me with light and truth be blessed,
> Be these the guides to lead the way
> Till, as on Holy hill, I rest."

Yet he who " would fain find Right, would fain shun Wrong," as on a holy hill walks every day.

Yes, care must be taken. We must not do harm in seeking to do good. But this scarcely justifies us in refusing to study how harm may be avoided and good effected.

If, in pursuing a general principle, one, " as one led by a way " unsought for, finds, with surprise, much is being said that was never originally intended, and where there was no personal call to say anything (indeed, far otherwise), that must be taken as the chance fate of the moment, and because Religious Freedom is already established in most parts of the world, and these, those generally called the most enlightened, political freedom is established in many of them, freedom of trade in some of them, and so on ; while again what ",withes that bind " the future will seek to loosen, is still the secret of the future. Armies may disband, swords be beaten into pruning-hooks, antique ideals be fulfilled. The fact that those ideals exist, is indeed a sort of promise of their fulfilment. Man will not stop until his highest ideal is reached. And, with each eminence attained, new heights beyond will soar. To-day we see some hill, next beyond us, about, as it were, to melt away, surmounted by the onward tread of the race. But what name the hill bears, only in a secondary way at all interests me. What interests me is the progress of mankind, a progress which makes the tears by the waters of Babylon, the weeping voice in Rama, the anguishes of the past—past. Past and never to return—as far as we can see.

After progression, retrogression ? After gradation, degradation ? Well, that is a long way off, we hope. The higher we go now, the further off. Yes, " the hopeless vulgarity of the human race " will press close upon, and trip up the heels of, almost all progress—if we are not on our guard, we and those to come after us.

A LOOKER-ON IN VIENNA.

PRELUDE.

Backward and forward swings
  the pendulum, the soul.
Is it the soul of the past and the distant,
  Civilizations, cities, types,
  Great deeds, words, things exceptional,
  fair, quaint, or mysterious,
  Such as aye are portrayed by great masks,
  And the crowd of the maskers behind them,
  from our day to Job; or is 't only
  the soul of but everyday lives
  in our vanishing moment of time?

      With all, great and small,
      Of it conscious, unconscious,
      Still backward and forward,
        Backward and forward,
        The pendulum swings.

Is it the soul of the disappointed
  but not faithless wife,
  in the dull old Quaker-settled
  prairie town, following in
  imagination her only
  "twice-seen" artist lover
  through far lands; yet putting
  herself in his place, herself—
  who older, not so fair nor gifted,
  would be forever faithful?

Or is it the soul of the wandering
  light-hearted but not faithless husband,
  recalling the pretty, gentle,
  type-writer, so unconventional
  but so confiding and innocent?

Or is it the soul of the *devot*,
  seen when on the pilgrimage,
  so faith-bound yet passionate?

Or is it the soul of the clergyman,
   travelling with his little children
   and invalid wife—a soul
   beginning to expand a little ?

Or is it the soul of the constant
   inconstant husband, forever
   swinging back to the perfect wife ?

Or is it the soul of the dreaming
   moralist, picturing the vanity
   of every conception of unbridled pleasure ?

Or but some idealist's visions, material
   and mental and spiritual ?

Or is the pendulum swinging,
   as from hand to hand, across
   the stained table and half-emptied
   cups of the garrulous gaffers ?

Or is it from youth to age the
   pendulum swings ?
Or from pleasures to pains ?
Or from griefs turned to blessings ?

Or swings it but over the flow'rets,
   bay-bloom and iris commingled ?
Or through perfume of far-off acacias
   that over some river comes wafted ?
Or nigh-fluttering wings of the lovers,
   the night-moths that entered my chamber ?
Or where painted shells murmur tales
   of all climes and all races of beings ?
Or only through mist, from the smoke
   of the lamps when the flowers have faded.
Or marks it your beatings, old friend,
   soon to still, I mistake for a message ?
Or tells it each heart's ardent need
   of renouncement, devotion, adoring ?

'Twixt believing and doubting,
'Twixt gaining and losing,
'Twixt shunning and loving,
'Twixt wounds and 'twixt blessings.
'Twixt dreaming and waking,
'Twixt sight and unseeing,
Who shall praise? who shall blame?
Who shall doubt or affirm?

In silence, in singing,
Slow plodding, onwinging.
Not caring, or weighing,
Desponding, or hoping,
What e'er the soul's choosing
(Not choosing, or choosing,)—
Our part with the blessèd
The best part of life lost,
The truth conscience whispers.
As seed 'neath the harrow
Our all a last offering:
Not our way. the best way,—
In whatever system
Past, present, or future,
As gainer, or victim,
Not seeing, or seeing,
Portraying, forgetting.
Affirming, or doubting,
All blessings still seeking,
Passeth man's life
As a perfume, a vapor,
A thistledown floating
Through sunlight and shadow.
While backward and forward,
      Backward and forward,
The pendulum swings
Till the summer is over.

AGRALÄIDE.

LUKE 7 : 47

By R. A. E.

AGRALÄIDE.

SUBMISSION.

When the hours of day are passed,
And my work is laid aside,
And I watch a fading west
Where late the clouds were purple dyed,
Oft I ask where can he be,
And I wonder wistfully;
Wonder, wonder, wistfully,
Wondering ever —asking never
Does he ever think of me ?

Often in the silent night,
One beside me wrapt in sleep,
One sunk back from my embrace,
Sunk back into slumbers deep,
I look out across the dark,
As across a waveless sea,
Wondering where he may be;
Wond'ring more, yet asking ne'er
Does he ever think of me ?

O, thou sweet and sweet and dear !
Be thou far or be thou near,
Thine the smile and mine the tear.

Thine the joy of finding love
Where it pleaseth thee to rove,
Like a flower in a grove.

Mine to bear the flowret's tear,
Mine the pain of loving—Dear,
Pardon ! Ah, he cannot hear.

Thine the right, and mine the righting ;
Thine the love, and mine the loving ;
Thine the gift, and mine the giving.

Hush ! I through the darkness trace,
Soft ! Each feature of thy face,
Faint and misty, far away.

Dark thine eyes and soft and sweet,
Through the darkness, mine they greet,
Grave and tender, as thou sweet.

Underneath the parted shade
That hides the heaven of thy mouth
Ambush zephyrs of the south.

O'er the clear pale of thy cheek,
So soft and cool, with flying feet
A little blush plays hide and seek,

While my words of passion tell
Of the truth hid in the well
Into which thine image fell,

Yet thou hearing art so still,
That I love thee 'gainst my will,
Thou it will'st not, willing still.

Sweet, in being thou art best,
Thou art perfectest in rest;
Let my fancy thee invest

With each virtue ever known—
Lacking all, thou hast this one,
Thou hast made me all thine own.

Bad or good, I know but this,
In my life's-time perfect bliss
I have known but once—thy kiss.

Faintly, faintly through the night,
Fades thine image out of sight,
Faint come streaks of morning light.

O, my love! In my embrace,
Let the balm of thy dear face
Wrong of wasted life efface.

Gone! So best ; I called thee not,
I strive rather thee to blot
From my breast, full tried, God wot.

So I close my eyes to rest,
Lost in sleep my weary breast—
[In my dreams I see thee best.]

HALF A YEAR.

Half a year, oh ! my dear lost love,
Half a year since first I saw thee,
Since thou dawn'st, sweet star, making all light
A soul I knew not before was dark.

    Half a year, sweet, since, like islands perfume
      freighted,
    Sailing on southern seas, we drifted near
    —Oh ! my God—nearer, nearer !

Love we never spoke, and kissed.
But my yielding eyes, startled, wondering, uncon-
    scious,
For an instant seemed to ask, and thou reassuring,
    answered, " Only to be near each other ! "
    Sweet, all through life for those words
    I pray God's blessing on thee;
    On thy going out and coming in,
    On thee wholly and forever.

Sweet, if we escaped then, I know not what of sin;
Sweet, if we sinned then, in that second in I know
    not what ;
Sweet, though like barges that drift upon the tide,
We parted in the moment that we met, meeting
    were sundered
Not the less all the pain of life was in that instant
    paid.
Even sin condemning God, through an eternity of
    pain,
To punish this, me knowing wherefore I am pun-
    ished,
Must leave me memory of my sin, if it be sin,
So leave me bliss, in the memory of my bliss.
I cannot wholly wretched be again ; I have one in-
    stant lived ;
Henceforth I cannot know that living death which
    means death but to joy.
No future night will be so dark one ray of pure
    light will not reach through it.

Farewell, my love, my love, still my love, though
    I never see thee more in this life ;
This life ? Is there another where I shall see thee
    in joy or pain ?
Dear, hell would not be wholly hell with thee un-
    changed;
Thee changed, and heaven itself would not be
    heaven.
Farewell, sweet love ! Half a year of swift, lost
    life,
Since fate gave new revelation of the worth of life !
Half a year, and in all that time, only twice love,
Only twice thy lips were mine ; only twice, twin
    flowers of life !
Must life go on, half years be years, and years be
    life,
And like the aloe, flowering only once in all its life
I know no future joy but memory of past bliss ?

IN THE NIGHT WHEN THE HOUSE IS HUSHED.

In the night when the house is hushed
And all is still but my soul,
It goes forth to wing its way over the streets and
 lanes,
Over the fields and woods,
Over places where at midnight great forges flame,
 and through the night toil is;
Over the remnant of the land,
Over the trackless waste of waves,
Over the full sailed ships, like dim fair birds in the
 darkness below;
Or the steamer, with its many tiny points of light,
 teeming with human beings,
Each with its concentrated interests, is overtaken,
 felt, so close at hand, and passed,
[Are those specks open boats of wrecked men far
 from any land?]
Over cities, harbors of sin,
Over prairies silent under the moon,
Over rolling plains, Indian bands o'er-roven, and by
 herds of wild animals;
By grottos of hidden gold in ravines of arid moun-
 tains where few men have ever been;
By verdant vales with wondrous growths,
By all, by all, oh! my love, between me and thee;
Thee, thy lips so sweet in dreams,
Thy tender breast, thy gently encircling arms,
Thee! my goal, my shore, my abiding city.
Perhaps thou hast forgotten me, or even drivest me
 more than indifferent from thy thoughts;
Thou carest not for me; could I really meet thee
 thou mightest not care to be kind.
Dear love, in my thought thou art ever gentle as of
 yore,
O, my love, thou art still! O, God, art all my love.

Farewell beloved, till the starry hours
Which steep the world in sleep, say to my soul,
Behold again the hours when thy soul may seek,
And finding, fold its happy tired wings
Upon his perfumed breast.

THROUGH THE CROWDED STREETS.

Through the crowded streets I go;
All alone I seem—a stranger in the great city, and
  strange,
Far from home, from friendly greeting, native
  speech;
Yet there is one ever beside me.
Behold the piles of wealth and art!
I whisper to him all my thought.
I lose him in the hurrying rush and danger;
A moment only, now he is by my side again, silent,
  sweet invisible.
His hand slips into my hand,
My closing fingers touch his so dear palm,
His arm rests soft in mine.
All down my side is felt his gentle presence;
He returns a thousand and a thousand times,
And, in tender pity for my loss of him he images,
Is his image present, invisible, and ever faithful.

UNTO THE SPLENDID CAPITAL.

Unto the splendid capital of sin
I pilgrim came as to a sacred shrine.
They who seek shrines seek rest of soul,
To lay some burden down of sin or care,
To find some talisman 'gainst future pain,
And seeking, tribute pay in faith and praise.
So mine like praise, since mine like faith,
I sought there talisman to cure
Love's wasting fever in my heart,
To lay some burthen down—nepenthe find,
Forgetfulness of one too dear !
Ah! vain essay! behind soft eyes thine softer shone,
No lips are dear but thine in all the world
Who won my kiss won not 'twas given to thee.
Since I am wholly thine, or what or where I am,
And thou imperial o'er my soul, cruel or kind
I will not struggle more in vain emprise
Striking ajar the music of my thought
But patient take my sad sweet burden up,
And never hope to lay it down again,
Well paid by one short hour of bliss
For an eternity of pain.

HIS NAME IN FLOWERS.

I.

Oh! sweet Agral! Here let me write thy name,
    In characters of flowers,
As thou as fair as perishable.

II.

I said not characters of light.
The brilliant deed enthroned of fame,
The high achievement winning men's applause,
These are not thine or e'er will be,
Oh! bay flower of the wild sweet wood
Born but to be not do,
But being to be being wholly beautiful,
So I do fitly write thy name in flowers.

III.

I said not characters of flame.
The lofty sacrifice, the burning zeal
The priceless consecration unreserved to high
    ideal,
These not thy part, yet God made thee,
And made thee perfect for assignéd part
As whose ensample might have power
To change the faith of worlds ;
So full of tender reverence
I write thy name in flowers not flames.

IV.

Oh! that I had Horatio's pen
    To write thee fitly fair,
A monument as bronze enduring;
    Oh! that I had a tongue of fire
To sing thy sweet completeness in a song
As flowers all fair, far-reaching as the light,
And burning with my love's undying flame.

V.

The fairest flowers, and thy completeness, and
    these lines
        Haste each to perish soonest.
    Yet as arbutus blooms breath sweet
Beneath last year's dead leaves,
So I would have that fair that sings of thee ;
Although they never struggle to the light,
Or 'neath the waste of interests of the hour
Are born to be forgot, yet sweet Agral,
Though no eye see these lines thou art their
    theme,
So I would have them fair as flowers and light
    and flames.

VI.

Can they be else than fair sprung from my love
    and thee?
Could thy rare beauty's offspring be not beauti-
    ful,
Or love like mine find utterance not fair?
Alas! love makes not fair, else had I been
To thee as thou to me. So come dear flowers
For ye are fair, ah! ye are fair,
And weave my darling's coronal.

VII.

Dear love, when I would fitly write
    Thy darling name in flowers,
Beings like thee, born to be beautiful,
And so in being best—for beauty prized
Not med'cine worth—what flowers my choice?
What roses damascene can breath thy sweet,
What lotus dreaming on the golden Nile
    Can match thy perfumed calm?

VIII.

Not daffodils, nor eglantine, iris, nor **violets**
    meseem thy flowers,
Nor hair-bell's grace, nor yucca's stateliness,
Nor tulip's pride, nor daisy's modesty,
Nor lily of the valley's purity,
Nor homely hawthorne blooming fair
In English hedges in the spring,
Nor purple lilac's wealth of perfumed plumes,
Nor apple blossoms, ah! one May so dear.
—But jasmine, and cape jessamine,
Egyptian lotus and the daphnia's bloom,
Wax flowers, bay flowers, all magnolia blooms,
—Those most that mid their crowns of green
So smooth and cool, lift milky chalices
With odors over-running to the sun
Through all the pathless piney southern **woods**—
These seem like thee and thou like those,
Lancastrian roses twined between.

IX.

Then let me, leaving still unrobbed
The lily crown that bound the brows
Worthy to win imperial love,
One petal take to lay on thine
From brows that bound all perfectness
In one sweet bundle. Love, though thou
Could'st not give life for thy beloved
More than I could imperial be,
I did not love thee for thy nobleness—
I said not characters of light.

X,

Oh! come dear flowers and bring your perfectest
To bind his brows that doth outperfect your per-
    fection.
    Pay him the homage which is just,
Since ye are fair be second to his fairer.
Come sweetest buds and weave his coronal
Whom I did meet in his sweet manhood's
    fairest prime,
    Its perfect hour,
E'er his dear budding time had passed utterly.
Come fair corollas in your hour supreme,
Come in love's moment all divine,
    Your beauties all disclosing,
    Your sweetest sweets distilling,
    Your hour of perfumed joy,
Yet 'ere your rounded lines have lost
All sweet suggestion of your gracious budding
    time.

XI.

    [Oh! hour divine!
    Oh! half-blown rose of life!
What form so marred but thou hast glorified,
What life so mean but thou   hast sanctified?
Oh half blown rose of life
Love's hour divine,
Come lay thy chalice close to mine
That I may drink thy sweetness and become
    As fair as thou!
So—cup to cup, so—lip to lip ;
Now is thy rose come crimson in my veins,
I glow with beauty in thy beauty's glow,
Deepening thy tints in passionate response—
Thy sweet my sweeter answers more intoxicate
So that thou almost diest in my arms
The while I faint in thine.
[Who saw me grief-struck marred and beautiless,
And bent down o'er me as a princess o'er a king,
And won me back to beauty in his tender arms?]
Lo! When I meet one in that hour divine
I die before him as a lamp goes out
Before the throne of God.
Oh! Light eneffable that shines for me
Why should I shame that I am that thou mad'st?
I can not tell whence comes or goes that force
    divine
Divine! I only knew it that it masters mine.]

As 1 came down the terraced stairs
That scale the Pincio to the Trinita,
And, pausing 'gainst the balustrade,
Look'd far toward the wondrous dome
Ruling the Roman night,
I heard a voice so still, so near,
Where no one was, that answered mine,
I heard the voice of him I loved
Afar beyond the sea—

So still, so near, so sweet, so far !

The years have gone, but still I hear
The quiet sweetness of that word
In the still Roman night.
The sweetness hear, but can not tell
The word, if 'ere I knew.
I sometimes think that so the scene
Is symbol of my life.
Afar from thine my lot is cast—
Afar in thought, in hopes, in cares,—
The rolling leagues of space between
Dividing least.
Fate's purpose when thy life edged mine
'Tis as a half caught word—one word—
Whose meaning I shall never know,
But whose sweet music, stillest in stillest night
Is ever with me. And these lines
Are half-caught echoes of that music—meaning
    what they may—
Music that still comes back as life speeds on
Far from the past and thee.

Lo ! I have named the flowers that spell thy
    name, yet know
These lines are flowers, such as the fates have
    willed,
Sprung from the plant thou bad'st to bloom
Nor bidding knew thou bad'st.
This book the withe that binds them
They who read, if any e'er,
And disentwine them, they shall here
Thy name emburied find, my sweet Agral
And writ in flowers.

LAST NIGHT I LAY UPON MY BED.

Last night I lay upon my bed
And prayed to Jesu 'ere I went to sleep,
And in that moment elevate,
Of faith supreme, acceptive, self-negate,
As mists that part and leave the rock revealed
The tissue parted of old prejudice,
    Notions of nature nature gives the lie to every
      day,
    Utterings of them that dream, and dream
    The echoes of their dreams God's law,
    Created and unnatural shame—a shame
    Offspring of what is artificial, so a shame
    God's other creatures, nature's children, never
      know,—
    A tissue shot with fears : first, of man's scorn,
  Despising what he knows not therefore scorns,
  Then penalties enact of them would hide
  Themselves are forfeit to the laws they made,
  Then fear of dread hereafter and God's wrath
  Because they were the creatures that he made,
All parted, like a vesture overworn,
    And from afar,
    Yet seen so near
    In the sweet light of prayer,
The truth eternal standing there
Look'd back—looked deep into my eyes
    And wou'd be known.

ALL THROUGH THE NIGHT THE SOFT SOUTH WESTERN WIND.

All through the night the soft south western wind
  Breathed from the sea,
  And at my opened lattice bars,
  Beating with whispers soft and wakening me,
  Called me, from dreams of thee, to thee
  Oh! new found love, to thee!

Lo! as some full sailed argosy
Freighted with echoes from the land of dreams
  I floated back to sense,
Through the sweet portals of half consciousness.
  A wondering sense of joy and love
  And peace filled all the room,
A joy I woke to, still part echo of past joy,
And circling, nestled fluttering down upon my
    breast.

  I could not rest
But through the darkness stole, and longing, happy,
    Lean'd out to the night.
  Far below the drifting light
  Showed where the deep laid barges moved
  That floated on the silent tide
The stillness made more still with whispering leaves,
The far-off breath of ferns, the sense impalpable
Of purity delicious of the night amidst the hills.
The setting stars, and love, love come at last
  After so many years.

  In the long day which followed,
  After the night divine though night alone,
  I read his sonnets in the rose-hung porch
  Who sang a love like mine,
  Yet ever fitful starting back
To seek through rooms deserted for the love I knew
  was far away.

It was a Sunday, all the world at rest,
  And in my heart loves flowret bloomed
  To leave me restless ever more.

  How strange my dual life that day,
  Each questioner answering, seeming custom's
    self,
  Yet every present moment absent with my love.

In the late afternoon we wandered through the
    shaded lanes to church.
How short the sermon seemed, the old priest eloquent
And when they sang Magnificat, dear God, forgive
  If love took up the sacred strain,
  The organ and my voice in unison,
Till the quaint rafters rang with melody.

  Oh! night and day divine, all sweet,
  The whole of life till thee led up to thee,
  The whole of life since thee thy memory.

AGRAL.

(Recallings.)

Out of the dark and the turmoil I found thee,
Out of the smoke and the clangor and din.
And you coming, all changed to me. Silent an iris
Her lilies leans tow'rd thee, as over still waters.
All changes. A perfume of flow'rets breathes 'round me,
A perfume of flow'rets breathes round me and stills me,
And in thy repose, as one wrapt, lost, an iris,
By the margin of waters, beholds thee as moonlight
Asleep on the flow'rs, or the first star of ev'ning,
Or where in the moonlight two white doves are sleeping,
(Stiller thyself in thy stillness than sleeping)
Beheld thee and yielded, thee follow'd with perfumes,
Lean'd tow'rd thee, half touch'd thee, and O, o'er the waters,
The waters between us, would draw thee, adoring.

You saw me. You lov'd me? I know not. You took me;
In your bosom did fold me. I rest there encrowned.
Your love than all crowns, fame, or fortune, is sweeter,
More worth, more ennobling, more staying, more stilling.

Lean over the waters your chalice of silver
O lotus, O lily, O bay flower emperfumed,
Lean over the waters, O monarch, and bind me.

You bid me, you bind me, breathe on me, and bind me;
I die, in twice living; I cease, in beginning;
Life opens, in yielding my life unto thine.
You crown, in discrowning me; bless, in destroying me;
Make, in unmaking me; free me, in binding me.
Lo! I all abdicate, yield all my prizèd most;
Find in my conqueror all my rewarding,
And sink in the arms of that conqu'ror adoring,
All yielding, all finding, all learn'd, all forgetting.

O conqueror all conquering, the bay leaves are calling,
The flag leaves of sweetness are calling and trembling.
Is night gone? Is't morning? The song birds of morning
  Call us and call us.
                   You heed not? I heed not.
I follow your motions. I still me when you are still.
  Lo, I am wedded. I lose power of motion.
  (Self will was priz'd once. How strange! I no will have now.)
Sing softly sweet songsters. Hush, wakèn no lovers.

By the margin of waters, cool waters, a marriage
  Hath someone befallen, and someone is blessed now,
    Someone is blessèd now, . . . blessèd now, .
      blessèd.

  Soft and more softly as morning advances
Dies the song into silence, a silence unending,
  Sweeter than song, and to end never more.

Lo, now the iris blooms sweet all the waters by.
Nay not as yesterday, nay not as yesterday.
Why not as yesterday? Why not as yesterday?
  O purple petals, as frail in the wind now
As ever, yet sweetened thy pèrfume with pèrfumes
  Borne from his lips, even borne to thine inmost heart,
(I bear in my bosom his likeness, his pèrfume;
I bear in my bosom his likeness, his sweetest self.
  Soft! Are they singing still? Is it that morning?)
  O purple petals, so frail in the wind there,
Unfolding so free, though so frail, so uncaring,
  There, by the waters, sang you as larks sing,—
Sang you as bob-o'-links in the June meadows,
  There, where they swing on the grass ere the mowing,
  There, where they swing on the grain ere its ripening,
  Pour forth their song, full of joy, free of thought or care,
Full of joy in so living, in filling their metier,
  Joyous and passionless, (painless their passions all),—
  There, by the waters, sang you as larks sing,
  Sang you as bob-o'-links in the June meadows.

Sing you as nightingales now in the evening;
Press 'gainst the thorn, the sweet thorn, your breast's aching;
Sing of love's sting, love's awak'ning and crowning;
Sing of love's sting; and so sing evermore.

Still, still the iris blooms, blooms by sweet waters there,
By the same waters blooms, blooms there as yesterday,
Opens its petals so frail in the wind there,—
But not as yesterday, ne'ermore as yesterday.

Rude stalk and sword-like leaves, breaking when least weights
    press,
Mystery of tints of the heart of the flower,
O pistils and stamens, and petals uneven
Yet rhythmic, set symbols of triads, O Iris,
Discrownèd forever and now ever crownèd!

He lean'd neath the stars in the dark 'cross the water
And breathed on the chalice. The chalice bent tow'rds him.
Its lips, yielding, longing, empèrfumed, he pèrfumes.

Behold me. Consign to me.
Love's crown assign to me.
His chosen! His servant! His liv'ry now bind on me.
O, best gift of life, life half over, assign'd to me!
Love hath found me, and crown'd me, and, joy of all, bound me.

O self-willing, priz'd once, I'm rich finding quits of thee.
Who was so frail, blooming free by the water side?
Strong of root, rude of stalk, frail of petal, an iris?
(Frail of petal, an iris; frail, frail, an iris!)

THE SOLDAN.

An eastern Soldan had a favorite slave
He bound about with gems and with his royal love.
And full of gratitude she lived content,
Until one sad sweet day strange fate,
That ever toys with human griefs and joys,
Embrasure made in custom's wall
That hedges Indian wives—she saw, and loved,
Was seen, beloved—more blest than I.
Some stolen interchange, wordless but love translate
A signal and a silken rope.
Flight and discovery, and then fierce pursuit.
O'ertaken on a river's bank
Lashed by a swollen flood,
Escape cut off—the nearing horsemen from afar
Shouted their soldan's word of grace,
Forgiveness, and return.
Return is parted life,
Sweeter is death with love ;
Each took one long dear look,
Then plunged into the flo d,
And perished in the other's arms.
Later the tired, sated waves
Laid soft the lovers' forms on stream-lapped strand,
Bruised and stripped, but beautiful in death,
And in that last embrace still locked.
And there the noble Soldan raised
A splendid fane, set fair with lazuli,
And rich with traceries of eastern art,
And graved it with the story of their fate,
So that there might not perish from the earth,
The memory of so much love ;
And wrote these words upon the crowning stone
" SOLDAN THE MIGHTY UNTO LOVE SUPREME."

IN ITALY.

When I see these golden hills,
 All their sweetness knowing,
When their strange wild perfume fills
 All my senses softly blowing
From the terraces of vines,
 When these ancient rocks the sun
 Crimsons 'ere the day is done,—
Topaz, ruby, amethyst,
Sweetest hues like lover's tryst
 Given and taken,—
 Loved, forsaken,
My heart goes back across the sea.
Sweetest of all sweets to me
Could I wander them with thee
Sweeter sweet these hills would be.

When through olive boughs the sky
 Azure depths revealing,
Watching dreamily I lie,
 While faint sounds of life come stealing
From the valley far below,
 When beneath the o'er-reaching shade
 Afar flash crysop, turquoise, jade,
Where as azure waves break white
On a shore of gold, hues bright
 Given and taken,
 Loved, forsaken,
My heart goes back across the sea.
Gem of gems could'st thou with me
Watch this sky and flashing sea,
Sea and sky would brighter be.

When the city of a dream,
   Throned on emeralds, drifting,
Floats upon the silver sheen,
   All her misty domes uplifting
Through the silence of the night,
   When her torches flame afar,
   And is borne upon the air
Sounds of music, where no feet
'Ere have echoed through a street,
   Oh, love waken!
      Thee forsaken
What are dreams of light to me?
Music is not without thee!
Dreams of light and music be
In thine arms beyond the sea.

Way-worn in some house of prayer
   At the day's close kneeling,
Though the crucifix is there,
   Present help, a thought comes stealing
Of thee love so far away.
   So I close my book of prayer,
   For I see but thy name there,
And I cry, oh! make of me
What thou would'st, Lord, I should be!
   Truth o'ertaken
      I awaken,
Tears of joy break forth from me!
Thy life my love are purity,
And through all eternity
God smiles on my love for thee.

FINIS.

SUITE : THE EGLANTINE.

I.

THE EGLANTINE.

As I passed through the wild wooded pathway,
    I, with a crowd of the elegant,
    Came we on eglantine roses,
    There in a shaded place blooming.
    Who else remarked them I know not,
    I though, remarked them, and softly
    Smiled to myself, for I minded
    One who to me was known only,
    One who for me was then waiting.
    One who from many companions
    Me gently chose, and had waited
    Oft in a shadowed place for me ;
    Waited that we two might wander
    Aimless, but happy together,
    Talking, or silent, together,
    Leaving the crowded streets never
    'Till it grew late, and then parting
    With but a hand's pressure only ;
    Knowing not even each other
By name, or if ever each other
We lost, how to find one another ;

    One of a singular beauty,
    Whose lips were like eglantine petals,
And whose hair from her forehead all golden
    Fell back like its clustering stamens ;
    Tall and of elegant build,
    Beautifully formed and yet slender,
    Gracious in carriage and proud,
    Serious, full of refinement,
    And so like an eglantine rose
That, at sight of its namesake, I whispered,
    Smiling and silent and happy :

I have an eglantine rose
Waiting for me as its lover,
Waiting for me in its beauty,
In its sweet budding perfection;
Mine its pink petals, its stamens,
Its delicate perfume, its summer,
Mine the sweet joy of possession,
And the hope of the coming hereafter ;
And for me it is waiting, is waiting.
O for me, O for me, it is waiting.

And thence forward the way was all sweeter,
Life with its sorrows made happier,
And they that walked with me were fairer,
And they that walked with me were happier,
Sharing my mood, but not dreaming what caused it.

Ah, my dear eglantine rose,
Sweet is to-day.   And to-morrow ?
Nay, I will pray and not borrow :
Thine be the thorn, mine the sorrow.

II.

THE EGLANTINE TO ITSELF.

A Blossom.

" Seek not for lovers more than this ;
Thou coulds't not, if thou would'st, increase the bliss
That now attends thee, Eglantine.
Unnoticed by the way-side, and alone,
Thine was a life of waiting.   Came
At last this dear one with a lover's claim,
And took thee home and gave thee rest.
There, in love's arms of snowy white,
Loving, tender, passionate,

Pillowed upon that faithful breast,
Be thou content from all the rest
To separate, and dream on thus forever."

III.

THE EGLANTINE TO ITS LOVER.

A Blossom.

" 'Till first we met, within my heart
  There was an aching void unfilled :
But, by thy magic power t' impart
  Command, its wild unrest is stilled.
O love me with a friendship pure,
  That shall through darkest hours abide,
Through every trial of faith endure ;
  Be thou mine always, till the tide
Of life is at its ebb, and we
  Launched forth into eternity."

IV.

THE EGLANTINE ON THE MOUNTAIN SIDE.

A Blossom.

I watched at night with the charcoal burners
    Close by their smouldering fires.
They were farmers' sons from the valley below,
    And watched well their smouldering fires.
And among them were lovers. Hush! softly the night wind
    Fanning the smouldering fires.
Kisses the lovers there. I had a lover there,
    There by the smouldering fires,
And my lover and I watched faithfully, wakefully,
Under the solemn stars, faithfully, wakefully,
    Night long the smouldering fires.

V.

IN THE CITY.

[JUNE IS SWIFTLY PASSING.]

I saw you to-day, to-day on the prado,
But you were in cloud land fair, evidently,
And did not perceive the poor little mortal
Whose heart to her throat leap'd at sight of her loved one.

I dared not to speak to you, dear one, so near me,
Nor scarce dared to look toward the one I so loved ;
Ah ! dared not.   But oh ! by my heart's beating, throbbing,
I know, I can swear : still the eglantine lives.

JUNE.

Soon, ah! too soon the unnumbered days,
Flying with roseate feet their ways,
Leave us. The dark month longest stays :
   The sweetest month is still the shortest.

In June the Eglantine alone
May bloom, alas! When June is done,
For other flowrets smiles the sun.
   Farewell, sweet June, of months the shortest.

VII.

REASON.

You number of each month the days,
And say, June 'tis not shortest stays.
I know, dear; you are right always;
   For you, no month wounds, none is shortest.

But eglantines bloom in but one.
O, when thy light is gone, my sun,
My June is o'er, my summer done:
   My one sweet month has been my shortest.

VIII.

SWEET IMPRESSIONS ARE THE LONGEST LASTING.

Few are the days to which 'tis given to trace
Lines which the coming years will not efface.

Many the years whose whole united power,
Graves not a line so deep as one short hour.

Pass swift the years, and as a wave washed strand
Not e'en a foot print leave they on the sand.

Yet, still beyond them, haply looking back,
Where one sweet hour or moment left a track,
See we the mark each time we turn about . . . .
These are the marks we would not have washed out.

IX

SWEET YEARS AWAY.

[On seeing an Eglantine rose in a little girl's album.]

Sweet years away,
One summer's day,
Across my way,
A slender spray
Of wild rose eglantine,
      Fate lightly drifted.

Scarce mine the flower
One summer hour,
Yet, (ah ! love's power !)
Now every flower
Of wild rose eglantine
      With spell is gifted.

" O shadows dense,
Care, grief, offense,
Spare innocence ;
Stay aye far hence !"
Whispers mine eglantine :
      Lo ! clouds are rifted,

And I a care
With angels share,
And on the air
A sigh of prayer,
Born of an eglantine,
      To Heaven is lifted.

X.
IN THE AIR SOMETIMES TOWARDS EVENING.

In the air, sometimes, toward evening,
In the street, or in crowds, or where hastening
Some whither, lightly across me
Falls a vague sense as of something
Fair, from the far past returning,
Floating the air in about me ;
Delicate, gentle. aerial,
Close by me, but like a melody
Listened to long ago somewhere,
Yet which escapes full recalling ;
Faint, evanescent, impalpable.
As o'er the river comes wafted
Borne on the airs of the evening
Sometimes the breath of acacias
Blooming in June, or of far off
Orange groves blooming in winter.

Always it charms, it surprises,
Floats by, caresses, escapes me ;
Then in a half wonder leaves me.
Then, haply just as 'tis passing
Out of my mind as past guessing,
Softly I find me, as years ago
There in the wild wooded pathway,
Smiling, and to myself gently.
While on my way I pass musing,
Whispering low : Eglantine !

[From Alessandro da Vanora.]

THREE WINDS.

[El devoto, loq.]

1.

THE EAST WIND.

The wind is East; desires dead:
I am enfranchis'd of a slavery.
This is a day to die and be with God;
For love remains, but Janus-faced, love's changed.
  To-day love's face shines pure as those
That dawn celestial from the golden doors
  The old monk painted long ago
And dreamed he drew the answers to his prayers,—
  [Nor err'd; save but by faith and prayer
Came 'ere conception of such purity.]

    All day the clouds hang low,
    Past or not come the storm;
    Through crowded streets I go
        As if alone;
    Not one of all I meet can stir my heart.
    Still and superior and apart
        I yet see all;
    Not condemning though I share not,
        Care not,
    Sympathize with not;
    Appreciating, pitying, but as one afar,
Untouch'd, unwounded, not myself concern'd,
Yet with a tender gracious pity such as far angels have,
        Sinless themselves,
    Accepting things ordain'd, and seeing sin as one
        Having its place.

This is a day to judge of other men's misdeeds,
        My own so far away.
Calm, unprejudging, but, the light of reason clear:
All knowledge mine, hate, sympathy, with none,
Not even my own knowledge or past deeds;

Knowing the threads linking all deeds to causes far remote :
Not repentant, not defending, seeing all the regrettable :
How far remote is life, midst life, to me, to-day !
   Your eyes turn'd on me sin inviting,
     Seeking, longing, I behold
     As if turn'd I ask not where ;
   Yet knowing all ; pitying your unrest ;
Thankful for my repose, my respite-like content.

A sense elegiac possesses me,
   Like minor chords with all the wail,
The discord, passion, discontent, left out.
Passionless, pure, belonging to no day or time.
      I pass upon my way :
   All ways alike to me to-day.

II.

THE CHANGING WIND.

The wind is changing. Oh, this restlessness !
   Almost I dare to throw myself
   Off from the ramparts of fair fame,
And herd with shadows in some quest unknown.
   Lo, hurry past me shadows dark,
Ready to lead me where I dare not think :
   I pressing on to get me clear
   The city's lights. More air, more air !
Yet here the night sky and the cooling wind.
They cannot satisfy, they fan my flame.
   Shall I give up my best ? My best !
   My best is this esteemèd worst.
   —Is not this best, this worst esteem'd ?—
   And others ? Save, O Crucified,
Oh, save ! . . . and crucify my life.

Homeward I come, my heart still torn,
Weary and worn out and forlorn,
Each step I tread as on a thorn.
Sleeps all the world ? I may not sleep.

I must to-night forc'd vigil keep,
Dragging my limbs as up a weary steep,
Using mine eyes as weary eyes that weep,
That see, yet see nought; oh, I may not sleep.
　E'en to disrobe I scarcely dare,
Fearing vague evil in God's world so fair.
So, 'till nigh morning comes, and I fall there
　On pallet bare, lose foul and fair
　In the dead slumber of despair.
In that strong slumber still wild fancy teems
Forbidding e'en the dreaming of sweet dreams.

III.

THE SOUTHWEST WIND.

The southwest wind breathes soft and love returns
From fairy islands in some far off sea.

I hear the plash of waves along the strand,
Of waves that break far out to sea and glide
In foamy reaches up the silver sands,—
Soft murmurs musical, from coral caves
Where waves break chamber'd in the azure dark.
And hist'ries are enact of strange despair,
Whose echoes, lingering on in whisper'd tones.
Are heard in painted shells from Indian seas.

Now, from the waving groves of palm, a band
Of Indian girls breaks fair, a-down the beach,
With jewel'd anklets gleaming in the sun.
The ripple of their laughter softly heard
Comes borne upon the zephyrs, while they move
In motion, mystic, rhythmic, unconfin'd,　　　'
Down to the swelling sea. Soft breathes the wind:
The kissing ripples wet their dusky feet;
They beckon me. Soft breathes the southwest wind.

SHALL I ever see again
Thy sweet presence, whose dear absence
In some hour of every day
Present is to me ? ah ! say,
Shall I ever see again,
E'er again those tender eyes,
Giving me a sweet surprise
Every time I saw their light ?
Eyes, ye were not very bright,
Large, nor lustrous : whence your power,
Soon but once, thus in some hour
Of every day, to bring to me,
Sweet eyes, your tender memory ?

Long ago in Portugal
Sang the Poet Camoëns,
Songs of love, and love's sweet pain,
In the breast of Camoëns,
Lingering, prisoned in his song,
Has thrilled the ages all along.
And, of all his songs, I ween
" Sweetest eyes were ever seen,"
Is the sweetest; and I know
Sweet were the eyes he named so :
Yet, I wonder, would he own,
Or not, thine sweeter, dear unknown ?

TO AN UNKNOWN.

On, sweetest, sweetest, dearest flower,
Rest on my breast a single hour,
    Exhale thy sweetness there,
    For thou art passing fair,
       And I would be
Lost in the bliss of breathing thee.

Then let me dream I too am fair,
That, in the bliss of bearing there
    So sweet a flower,
    I dream the hour
      As sweet to thee,
Lost in the bliss of breathing me.

CONFESSION.

"Love me little, love me long!"
So it runs, the old-time song,
And I sing it, but I know
In my heart I long not so.
No, I ask not for that rest!
Fling yourself upon my breast,
Clasp me in your arms and cry,
" 'Tis not you want rest, 'tis I."
Clasp me in your arms of fire,
Glowing you with love's desire ;
Melt my coldness in your flame,
Let its fuel be my blame
That I love not more, nor know
I love most when seeming snow.
Give me bliss by being blest,
Give me rest by finding rest ;
Let your head the livelong night
Rest upon my bosom white,
Feed on banks of lilies there,
While I, like a cloud in air,
Seem to float in azure space,
Locked and lost in your embrace.

But, if e'er a morrow bring
Not the love in you I sing,
If I lose you, let me not
Know my loss! be all forgot,
While, oh! fate, make thou of me
Lover's food perennially.

LAW.

Earth caught the flying night
And heldit in a long and sweet embrace :
Then morn arose, dewy and beautiful ;
Swift following like a burning lover came the Sun.
His rays fell on the sleeping flower ;
The flower, awakening, opened all his purple petals,
And bared its perfumed bosom to its Lord.
Then through the sunny air came her bee lover,
And burying him deep in the flow'ret's honied cup,
Drank deep the sweetness of its nectar-bearing breast.
Behold ! I said, the law of Life—the law of God—
In all my members, as in nature, striving,
Calling to sweet obedience ! Vainly strove
The Hebrew doctors of an ancient time
To make that law God had not made,—
To bind, as God's, laws not God-made.
Bind as ye will, nature breaks through,
All sweet unsufferance she proclaims God's law ;
And I obey—yield wise to fate,
Mine through all time—my fate—my fate !

Ἀνελπιστος.

I LIE upon the drifted sand,
The sea beats sadly on the strand,
Thy love is like a far off land.

The winds and waves, in concert drear,
Sob like lost souls in grief or fear,—
My cheek bears no repentant tear.

The stars unpitying hang on high,
No friend, no counsellor, is nigh,
Breaks from me one despairing cry.

A fitful light far out at sea
Shows haply some rich argosy,
What good can ever come to me ?

Lost innocence is mine at last,
The good once mine, late prized, is past,
And life is slipping from me fast.

Though wave on wave each nearer come,
Or near or far to me the same,
They cannot wash away my shame.

SHAME.

When Faith is dead, then Sin is naught,
A relic of an antique thought,
A name—ah! freedom dearly bought!

Though Sin be not, man's scorn remains,
The stigma of reproach still stains;
Despisèd!—ah! what good remains?

To know no word of scorn for you
Go undeserved, or false or true
The law of scorn, the scorn you rue.

FEAR.

Where "Faith" is all, there Truth is naught,
Delusion vain of "Modern Thought,"
A name with direst peril fraught.

Though Truth be not, conscience remains,
And insincerity still stains;
Led blindly—ah! what good remains?

Where conscience yields to human scorn,
How shall the soul of man be born
Anew, to greet the Judgment Morn?

FAITHFULNESS.

Yes, insincerity still stains,
And with sincerity remains
Loyalty ever, faith that knows no feigns.

O loyal, faithful brother, through the Night
Sigh not. Thou worshippest the Right.
Though dim the path, thy soul still walks in Light.

Who seeks the right, would fain shun wrong,
So turns from sin, and wakes his song
Each day in Heav'n his path along.

[And yet, perchance, oh, sweet surprise,
To me'll be given to ope mine eyes
And see my Lord beyond the skies!

Oh, vision sweet! as when, a child,
I dream'd, one night, my Saviour smiled,
Answering my question: Am I reconciled?]

I SAW MY LOVE A FAINTING LILY.

[FROM A BOOK OF DREAMS.]

I saw my love, a fainting lily,
In a garden where there were no other flowers:
Her beauty filled the place.
And from afar I seeing her, rushed eagerly,
Hungry to throw myself upon her snowy breast.
I was a blush rose dizzy with perfume ;
Flushed and burning,
I lay upon the bosom of my lily,
And drank in
Heaven.

LOVE'S CHAPLET.

FIRST FORM.

Behold the chaplet of my love :
  First, lilies to her purity;
  And, that they may be more like her, let them be water lilies,
  Which do trusting rest upon the bosom of the waves,
  As she upon the breast of her beloved ;
  And let them water lilies be of sweet perfume,
  Which being rock'd and toss'd by wind and wave,
  As she by storm and sorrow of this weary world,
  Only give forth more sweetness ;
  Then, violets to her earnestness,
  Blush roses to her passion,
  And snow drops to her humility ;
  Nor let there wanting be rosemary and rue
  And thyme and lavender, and such like humbler herbs,
  These be the week-day virtues of this working world ;—
  Then bind the whole with ivy,
  To show that all these virtues be eternal ;
            So,
Behold the chaplet of my love.

Behold the chaplet of my love!
First, lilies
To her purity,
More like her, let
Be, which rest
The waves as she
Of her beloved.
Water lilies be
Which being rocked
And wave as she
Of this weary world,
More sweetness still.
Her earnestness,
Her passion, and
For humility ;
There wanting be
And rosemary,
Fragrant lavender,
Herbs ; these be
Needed aye
Then bind the whole

And that they be
Then water lilies
Trusting upon
Upon the breast
And let them
Of sweet perfume
And tossed by wind
By storm and sorrow
Only give forth
Then violets to
Blush roses to
Bring snow-drops
Nor ever let
Marjoram, rue
Wild thyme and
And such like humbler
The week day virtues
I' the working world.

LOVE'S CHAPLET.

Behold the chaplet of my love,
My darling, fair as snow white dove,
Whose flowers I prize all blooms above.

First, lilies to her purity,
And that they be more like her, see
That they do water lilies be,

Which, floating on the wavelet's crest,
Or in its cradle, trusting rest,
As she upon the faithful breast

Of her beloved. And bid each bloom
That in my chaplet asketh room,
Be lily of as sweet perfume

As, seek how far so 'ere, I'd find ;
That, rocked or tossed by wave and wind,
As she by storm and sorrow blind

Oft i' the weary world, it will,
E'en though its cup the wavelets fill,
Only give forth more sweetness still.

Then, though all blooms her worth confess.
Blush roses to her passions stress,
And violets to her earnestness,

And snow drops for humility,
Bring most, nor let there wanting be
Or thyme, or rue, or rosemary,

And such like humbler herbs to show
The week-day virtues that we know,
This working world hath need of. So,

Now bind the whole with ivy, for
Though fade all flowers on time's sad shore,
Her virtues be for ever more.

ANGELUS.

[For a Triptych.]

Lo, the angelus is sounded,
  Calling faithful souls to prayer.
We thy faithful, love surrounded.
  Sing thee, one divinely fair:
    O te adoramus.

We thy lambs, O Shepherd gentle,
  Learn of greatest love through thine:
Thou hast in thy love parental
  Pour'd life's ichor out like wine:
    O te adoramus.

Those before the shrine are dreaming
  Of a Heaven beyond the sky:
Sweet, to us Heaven is no seeming.
  Heaven is where thou art nigh:
    O te adoramus.

O sweet Providence, stay with us:
  Life is death with thee not here;
Death is life with thee to share it:
  Losing thee our only fear:
    O te adoramus.

All sweet things of earth have ending:
  So thou, sweetest of her store.
Ah! if worth gave life unending,
  We should lose thee nevermore:
    O te adoramus.

If beyond the earth are angels,
  God and heaven beyond the sky,
Then, all angel, thou wilt reign there,
  Aye in thy fit company:
    O te adoramus.

We will live as thou would'st have us,
  What thee pleases God must please:
Then in heaven we shall before thee
  Sing in that eternal ease:
    O te adoramus.

Angel of God ! o'er all ascending,
O'er my heart's empire sceptre extending,
From thy serener realms tenderly bending,
    As with a mother's love
    Watching me from above,
    Thou tell'st a Heavenly dove,
      Angel of God.
        No more
    Doubt I a love divine.

Angel of God, past is deriding :
Lo ! where Angelico's sweet faith confiding,
Left on the golden doors record abiding,
    In every form and face
    Naught but divine I trace,
    Divine can not thine efface,
      Angel of God.
        Thou art,
    Therefore may angels be.

When all the host of heaven, legions of cherubim,
Rank upon rank upon rank, burning seraphim,
Martyrs, confessors and prophets all tell of Him,
    Lamb that was slain for thee,
    Worthy to reign for thee
    Through all eternity,
      Angel of God,
        Behold
    I see thee, and know the redeemèd.

Light in my darkest night steadfastly burning,
Shepherd and leader, true way at each turning,
Bread to my soul, wine of joy to my yearning,
  Though I no more than thee
  See, and adore but thee,
  Should'st thou implore for me,
   Angel of God,
    Thy merit,
  In need would atone for my blindness.

Late, when the river of death yawned to take me,
Despair, sin and doubt, with grief, banding to shake me,
In that dark hour love did not forsake me;
  Thou brought'st up from the flood
  By thy sheer faith in God,
  That whereupon trod,
   Angel of God,
    As firm
  As upon Peter's rock.

Yet had I fallen, so dizzied, O dearest one,
Hadst not thy guiding hand led me from stone to stone,
Up borne thyself as on air by thy faith alone.
  Yea I on safety's side,
  By bliss as sorrow tried,
  Had wandered, but my guide,
   Angel of God,
    Faithful,
  Still led me onward.

Now, to the All-comprehending, Invisible,
Powers conflicting, Triune, Indivisible,
Conscious or Unconscious, praise for thee visible.
  Mortal be thou, or more,
  Waif on the eternal's shore,
  We know not, but adore,
   Angel of God!
    In blessing.
  Sweet lives can never die.

Yet, if it ours be to choose our believing,
Mine, the sweet hope of my fathers receiving,
After earth, Heaven, all earth's errors retrieving.
    There, heaven to make complete,
    When I approach His feet,
    Thee waiting shall I meet,
        Angel of God. ,
          To lead
    Thy won up the silver stairs.

———

I.

O NUT brown eyes and golden hair
　　Made for your own and our undoing,
We can but wish we were so fair
　　And that 'twere you who did the wooing.

O roseate lips! The Eglantine
　　Hath breath less soft, hath hue less tender.
O, that our task were yours—to woo,
　　And it were ours but to surrender.

O, mossy touch! no velvet soft
　　Nor eider hath with thee comparing.
Ah! that your gift were ours, sweet one,
　　And we with you the gift were sharing.

Yes, yours the gift that none e'er tamed,
　　That wins unbid! Gift past extolling,
Gift still mysterious, still unnamed,
　　Though countless æons earth's been rolling.

O nut brown eyes and golden hair,
　　Made for your own and our undoing,
We met, we looked, we loved, we lived,
　　And neither knew which did the wooing.

II.

I read these words writ long ago,
　　And half I sigh, and half I'm smiling ;—
Was it a sin, that me beguiled,
　　Or gift from Heaven, that sweet beguiling ?

At eight, by Katie Saunder's side
　　I felt infantile ardor glowing ;
The decades pass. When will it stop,
　　This loving and this love bestowing ?

And more I smile that each new love
    Makes only all past love completer,
And all past love's completeness makes
    The last new love seem only sweeter.

III.

The autumn moonlight o'er my path
    Of fallen leaves soft shadows streweth ;
I count my fifty years and muse :—
    My cheek no tear regretful deweth.

I do not justify myself ;
    I yield mine all in full surrender
Unto the powers which make and keep,
    To whom I my account must render.

But, though I say not theirs the gift,
    I dare not say they not the giver,
Nor seemeth Heaven less pure that there
    I thee perchance may love forever.

IV.

O, nut brown eyes and golden hair !
    O dear lost past's divinest doing !
To meet, to look, to love, to live,
    And neither know which does the wooing.

AU CAFÉ.

I.

Breezy Old Buffer :

'Tis very sweet to be caress'd.
By old,—or young,—I like it best ;—
I like it best
To be caress'd.—
By plain, or fair ;
By one with hair
Like molten gold,—
Or ebon old
" That glitters blue-black in the sun."—
Or those that wear
A priceless wealth of auburn hair,—
Or those with locks less ample, still
Smoothly arranged,—or left at will.
Then, as to size,
What most I prize
Is tall,—or short,—
Or one that you
Would place somewhere betwixt the two,
And stout,—or slight.
Some when 'tis night,
Are fairer than they be by day ;
Then others, well, are fair alway ;
Others most fair by day, will lack
A certain charm when skies are black,
And mem'ry then can scarcely trace
The likeness of their daylight face.
Some are the fairest seen afar,
And other some are fairest near.
Some's charm's from strange, some native, sky.
Some please but once.   Some please for aye.
The bold, the shy, the grave, the gay,
Each pleases in her different way.

What I'd like most ? that you would know ?
—That I would scarcely like to show,
Lest what I named might seem to you
What none of taste would care to woo.
That'd do me wrong, my taste I mean,
Which, catholic, 's still nice I ween.
Stay ; I can make it clear to you,
My taste I can approve to you.
What would I win,
As well as woo ?
Well, I would like,—
Say, one that you
Would like to win,
And so would woo.

Come, boys and girls,
Old maids and churls,
Ye happy wives,
Men of blest lives,—
Come one, come all,
Confess, confess,—
'Tis very sweet a sweet caress.

CONTEMPLATIVE OLD BUFFER :

Each has his thought
Of what is best.
Caresses bought,
With bliss are fraught
To some, who call
Caresses, freely given, nought.
The best doth pall
On such as zest
Lack in all banquets,
And only find it in unrest.
Ah, happiest ye who
Love to give and take too !

PHILOSOPHIC OLD BUFFER :

Each, in his thought
Of what is best,

Choosing his own,
Should leave the rest,
And tolerate that others see
With eyes from his that different be.
What pleaseth 'pendeth on the pleased,
As sex and age is different seized,
Attracted, moved, and made to turn,
As moths that in the candle burn,
To'ard that which charms and fascinates,
Cools or consumes as will the fates.
Each positive its negative,
Each negative its positive,
Seeks and attracts as the decree
Of nature makes each need to be.
The need of each we all may know,
Judging by what their choices show.
Thus,—if their choice a proof we deem—
Unto their opposites 'twould seem
That boys are joys
And girls are pearls
And youths sweet truths.
And maidens fair
Delicious are,
And manhood bold
More worth than gold ;
And O, how good
Ripe womanhood !
To throbbing breast
All have a zest,
Each to his fellow.

Some like fruit mellow :
Others tart ; some sweet :
Some part company
Of those whose meat
On table's only tart or sweet.
The few I name,
Some would find tame ?
Well, I'll confess
That, truth to tell,

As for the rest,
By them as well
Some find it best
To be caress'd.
They find it best
To be caress'd:
It has a zest,
And makes them blest,
And gives them rest.

II.

COMPLACENT OLD BUFFER:

Since all are good,
Let who will meet
With all this day ;
Let me to-night ;
An 't suits my mood,
Meet her I've woo'd.
So, swift flies time
Till morning light.
Then let me be
As one at sea
Who sails to find
On some far sea
Rich argosy,
Or some night stand
On golden strand
Of promis'd land.

And so, ah so,
Let days on go,
Till I am old,
When all this gold,
In mem'ry stor'd,
Shall me afford
Rich dreams of past
Joys so amass'd ;
And serve me still,
The when I will,
In mem'ries sweet

Of banquets meet
For royal men.
On vain regrets,—
Ah! that most frets,—
For chances lost
I am not tost ;
For torture now,
And torture then,
Both to avoid
Is wise, I ween,
And never giving
When I feel like thrift.
So, never weary,
Would I make my shift ;
Storing my mem'ry and my strength by turns,
As nature bids,—to me reveals
Need of which rest my nature feels.
What hath most zest
To throbbing breast,
That most gives rest.
'Tis so to me ;
Haply to thee.

PRACTICAL OLD BUFFER :

Well, all you say
May be quite true ;
Some folk, no doubt,
Agree with you ;
But man was wise
To catch the prize
Nearest his hand ;
Rest to secure,
A wife and more.
Worth was the prize
Some sacrifice.   .   .

RADICAL OLD BUFFER :

.   .   .   Could none do better.
But are we
That backward he ?

Who profits most
By contracts, yet may most have lost.
Contracts and contracts be there ; more, less, cost.
Why should we be on question toss'd ?
Half truths are good, whole truths are better.
Wedlock is good ; but 'tis a fetter.
O, must I fetters wear ? 'Tis well,
Can I not walk without. Yet still
Who needs not crutch nor fetters must be held
Some better off than he
Who by their help may hobbledy
Just get along. In this age late,
The rough means of an earlier state
We sha'n't long use, to find in food
The fatherless. All means are good
Lead to good ends, till better, found,
Supplant them, sir ; as sickles were
To reap our fields, ere " Reapers " were
Made to reap fields faster and neater,
And give us bread plentier and sweeter.

SENTENTIOUS OLD BUFFER :

In days of old, black bread for Hodge ;
My lord might ride, but Hodge must trudge ;
White bread and railroads now ; for Hodge ?
There is no Hodge, and none need trudge.

III.

LONELY STRANGER AT THE NEXT TABLE :

Kellner, my reck'ning. Faugh ! their vile
Subject me chafes ; drives me off, while
I yet can't think what else to do.
Nor even think where'er to go.

IV.

WEARY WAITER (*sotto voce*) :

All gone ? Save these. Would they'd go too !
Their odious converse gives to me
A weary sense of vacancy.

I know them each ; and know they all
Profit by what they say 's a thrall.
Not one, if with his wife without,
Would know which way to turn about.
Who but their wives would ever look
At any of them twice ? Or brook
Their selfish egotistic talk—
Blague, most of it ? Or walk
Across the street for one, save she
So 'd get rid of his company ?
Old age, bereft of charm, is sad ;
Unwed, 'twould go all to the bad.
Bah ! here, a Hodge, I must wait up
While these old dolts, o'er empty cup,
Empty their empty heads,—of what ?—
Mere talk and froth and lies and rot.
I fain would go home to my wife,
But here am tied. Oh, this dog's life !
All gone but these, yet they sit here
And prate of what no one need fear
They think the tenth of what we hear,
Or know the thousandth part. Will ought
Ne'er stop these praters about nought,
Who should adjourn, let me instead
Shut up the place and go to bed ?

THE FIRST ODE FROM ANACREON.

I wished to sing of Atrides,
  Of Cadmus I wished to sing;
But still my lyre of love alone
  Responds with sounding string.

Lately indeed, I changed my strings
  And all my lyre, and I,
Fell singing the labors of Hercules,
  But my lyre would love reply.

Farewell to you then heroes,
  To you a long farewell,
For my lyre but on one theme,
  On the theme of love, shall dwell.

A NEW LOVE.

I have a love, and she is bonny,
  O how bonny, O how bonny,
As bonny as a love can be ;
And all that bonny is for me.
    For me ! for me !
    Ah ! can it be
That all that bonny is for me !

When she smiles the sky is azure ;
  O how azure, clear and azure,
As azure as a sky can be ;
And the sky smiles so for me.
    For me ! for me !
    Ah ! can it be
That the sky smiles so for me !

And her eyes they are like lode-stars,
  Burning lode-stars, tender lode-stars,
As full of love as eyes can be ;
And they glow with love for me!
    For me ! for me !
    Ah ! can it be
That that look of love's for me !

O tender eyes, and smile so fair,
And trembling lip, and rippling hair,
And mossy touch, have ye a care !
    The thought that ye are all for me,
    Its sweetness doth its bitter be,
    So sweet it breeds uncertainty.

THE MESSAGE.

DESERTED DAPHNE TO AN OLD LOVER.

Under the sea
Have travelled to thee
Words, and just three.

" Boy " and " both well."
What did that tell?
What did that spell?

Capital G,
R, A, N, D,
F, A and T,
H, E, R. See?

Grandfather? No!
Exactly, just so.
Grandfather. Oh!

What does that whisper,
That stings like a blister?
Of what truths consist, eh?

My high cocko'lorum
Must go in for decorum,
And in more than mere for-m;

Must consider how foolish
Are things done undulish;
And mustn't be mulish,

But meeting the fact, sir,
Must make a compact, sir,
Just how he must act, sir;

Mustn't run fast up-stairs,
Must shun knotty affairs,
Must abjure youthful airs;

Mustn't think his smiles pearls,
Nor his moustache give twirls,
Nor make eyes at the girls.

Each dog has his day,
And now old dog Tray
Must take grandfather's way ;

When walking abroad,
Must look at the road
And not at the crowd ;

And of sweet eyes to meet, or
For kisses still sweeter,
Or something completer,

No hope or thought ever
Must grandpa discover,
Or harbor. No, never.

And that friend like a lover
We each would discover
'Mid each crowd, must give over.

When that message to thee
Travelled under the sea,
To the past P. P. C.

AFTER ALL.

The schoolboy sings of love, love yet unknown;
The man a new love sings, the old scarce flown;
The grandsire sighs, his seeds of love all sown.
What for these several lovers can atone?

Is there atonement needed for the song?
Is there atonement needed, new love wrong?
Is there atonement needed, such seed sown?
Is there atonement needed when all's done?

Who answer brings convincing? Lo, march past
The Antique Faiths, each framed for aye to last;
They frown or smile from their experience vast,
While present ethics in new moulds are cast.

Things, praisèd once, are most detested late?
They may be prais'd again. Man's estimate
Of his suppos'd, real, needs at any date
Change with time's changing face. Wills Heav'n, or Fate?

Change too, men's estimate of written screed,
All ancient histories that bring, or breed,
Commandments, all authorities. Once freed
Such yoke, then for obedience blind what need?

Once for increase of warriors men took wives;
With peace, excess of men, scant food, man hives;
For health and wit, not numbers, then man strives,
For happier and more useful, longer lives.

Who wins love's happy; happier he who loves;
Happier yet he who loving, to love moves;
Happier who, full contented, never roves;
Happiest, such lover when earth, Heav'n, approves.

But what wins that approval? What is right?
Two things we have to guide us thro' the night
Of doubt: What through all parts brought most delight;
And conscience, answering to our cry for light.

The Future's order, our's? Their ways, our ways?
Man's erst best thought in no continuance stays;
Our virtues, sins may be in coming days;
Our sins worst thought of then have highest praise.

How shall we face our last hour, such words writ!
With bowèd head, in humble awe, as fit;
Yet soul serene, by light of conscience lit,
Victims to save aye still our powers knit.

Uttering conviction, victims save we'd fain,
Men's cruel automatic acts restrain,
Speaking as those who cried (alas, in vain!) :
Witchcraft's but naught, witch-fires but needless pain.

———————————————

Comes now the night, the night awaited long;
Fades now the light, the light that seem'd so strong;
Silent grows earth, earth once so full of song;
Joy mem'ries fade. Fade mem'ry too of wrong.

SUITE: AFTER THE SUMMER IS ENDED.

I. *'ΑΠΟΛΛΩΝ.*
II. THE LAST SIGH OF THE EXPIRING CONVOLVULUS.
III. THE SUNFLOWER.

'ΑΠΟΛΛΩΝ.

He was utterly beautiful,
And oh, when they saw Him,
Their souls from their bodies
Seemed to fall out, and to
Leave them defenceless,
And they to fall backward
As those dead before Him,
Their garments drop off them,
And leave them to lie,
A white offering before Him,
As fronting an altar.

He was girdled with lilies
And dripping with amber.
'Round his broad forehead
Was bound a gold coronal.
God-like, immortal,
Utterly beautiful,
He stood in his beauty
A conqueror triumphant.

Oh, dumbness of anguish,
Oh, chalice untasted,
Unutterable joys all denied them!
He saw them, yet saw them not,
Heard, as who hears not,
And smiling pass'd onward.

He smiled and I died.

He passed and I perished.

THE SUNFLOWER.

I saw
  On the floor
    Of the sky
    His chariot pass by.

    I cannot fly,
    I can only lie
  And adore,
    And keep my eye
      Turned to his light
      From morn to night.

And then not weep,
But sleep,
  To rest,
    For his dear sake,
    And 'gainst I wake,
  My aching breast,—
    (Sweet ache! sweet ache,
    That aches for his dear sake.)

Aching for love,
Of him above.
  More far,
    Than any star,
      More sweet,
      Than any meat,
        His sight,
        All my delight.

His fire
Kindles and puts out my desire.
The summer long,
He is my song.

Nor when the autumn comes do I complain,
That of my golden stamens none remain.
What were the need,
Now each a seed
Has full become
Quickened and pregnant with his love,
Each one the sum
Of all my good
Itself containing?
(I am not waning
When my seeds are ripe.
Then first my immortality's perchance begun.)

Each one the sum of all my good,
Quickened and pregnant with his love!
Ready when 'ere he calls me from above,
To wake from sleep,
As in his arms
Kept safe from harms,
And struggling to his light,
In all delight,
To sing again, again, again,
(As I his praise in glad refrain,
All summer long,
Have poured my song,
An endless strain,)
To sing again, again, again,
His endless praise in glad refrain,
While cycling ages wax and wane.

THE HIGH PRIEST.

I.

So stand, O great High Priest, upon the canvas limned,
In vesture sacerdotal of Melchisedec ;—
Yet more than priest, as thou, O Christ,
Art Priest and King. Purple for Royalty ;
Upon thy brows Mitre and Crown ;
Thine undervesture white in purity ;
Thy crimson robe ensanguined of the Sacrifice ;
About thy loins the golden girdle of Dominion bound ;
The mystic jewels of the Covenant
Made with the twelve, and us their heirs,
Once on thy shoulders as a burden borne,
Once as a lamb upon thy breast pressed close ;
Beneath thy feet the shadow of thy Cross ;
Thyself the Symbol of all sacrifice,
With outstretched hands that bear the Wounds ;
In azure air, eternal set, supernal seen,
Forever at the Father's throne
The incense of thine Intercession offering.

II.

(THE PICTURE.)

III.

As, when the painter rested from his work,
The poor, the ignorant, the race despised,
Journeying from far, forded the streams,
Threaded the forests where the bay flowers bloom ·
And, all unused to art, in wonder gazing,
Hush'd their rude voices in thy presence nor knew why,—
So when I come from howe'er far to thee,
Hush'd be the voices rude of daily life,
Of strife, of self-assertion, of complaint ;
Behind the symbol bid me see the symbolized ;
Be symbol of His love and of my fealty ;
Oh ! let thy jewels bear my name at last ;
And be my King ; forever be
Thine intercession's offering for me.

A DREAM.

I.

Wandering once in Italy,
    Glancing from the flying train,
Saw I wond'rous cupolas,—
    Seen, and never seen again.

Gray those ancient cupolas,
    Rising 'mid the towers, were seen,
Of an old wall'd city gray ;
    Green the valley all between.

Journeying oft in Italy,
    Glancing from the flying train,
Sought I oft those cupolas,
    Seen, and never seen again.

II.

In the crowded London street,
    On a sudden, wond'rous eyes
Fell on mine, as " Found at last ! "
    With a look of glad surprise.

Threading oft those crowded streets
    Sought I oft, behind, before,
The eyes I never can forget.
    But those eyes saw nevermore.

III.

Long years pass'd. Then, list, I dream'd
    Again I was in Italy,
And paus'd I where I saw afar
    Those ancient towers, green fields between.

Threaded I the verdant meads,
　　Nearing, found, without surprise,
Waiting for me, by the gate,
　　The owner of the wond'rous eyes.

We enter'd, hand in hand, the gate,
　　Pass'd silent through the ancient street,
Came where the vast cathedral stood,
　　Whose doors op'd to our entering feet.

O, wond'rous ancient cupola !
　　Its vast dome was of music made
And all its ancient galleries
　　Thrill'd sweet with: Love, be not afraid.

And Architecture vespers wove
　　That priests were chaunting, and I saw
Introit and benedicite
　　Rise solemn through the perfum'd air.

Its incense flow'rs, its flow'rs all sweet
　　Echoes of Eden's sacred rood ;
And lo, before the Patriarch,
　　We stood in innocence of God.

The Architecture while I hear,
　　While the gorgeous Music see,—
Lo, the ring was bless'd.   One speaks :
　　Seal'd at last and seal'd to me.

DIPTYCHS.

I.

Spring.

When the Spring is waning,
  Waxing into Summer,
Wherefore my complaining?
Waxing, it is gaining;
And gaining—why, gaining's gaining.
'Tis all the old retaining
And ever new attaining.
'Tis losing, that is paining.
Should aught but joy be reigning,
That sum of good obtaining
Of all old sweets remaining
And ever new attaining?
Then why this sad complaining,
All my present staining?
Ah! 'tis *Spring* is waning.

II.

Youth.

When our Youth is ended,—
  Into Manhood ripened—
Why with pride is blended
Aught of sadness? Ended
Is that which but offended.
The immature is ended,
To the mature ascended;
Imperfectness is mended;
The weakness, that contended
With perfect virtue, ended.
That we should feel offended,
Or sigh, like those unfriended,
O'er lack and fault amended,
Is not to be defended.

Aye! but *Youth* is ended.

THE GRIEF.

As in the Summer I sat singing,
  Singing, singing, singing, singing,
A Grief unto my heart came winging,
  A grief came winging to my heart.

    Wildly I rose with youth's grief fearing,
      My heart's defences bound about;
    And all my misery forescoing,
      Vainly strove to bar it out.

    But the grief whose wing was weary
      With long beating of the air,
    Forced an entrance to my heart,
      And having entered rested there.

In the Autumn I sat sighing,
  Sighing, sighing, sighing, sighing,
For the grief within my heart was dying,
  The grief was dying in my heart.

    Why then, I asked, this strange repining?
      Why sigh at loss of care and pain?
    This grief, my heart's rest undermining,
      Why almost wish it would remain?

    I who had opposed its coming,
      Suffered from it tears and care,
    From in my heart long bearing of it,
      Had learned to love it resting there.

LES CHAMPS ELYSÉES.

[A DEUX.]

I.

We sat beneath the chestnuts' leafy shade,
Beside the fountains garlanded with flowers,
In early summer, the full day begun;
Sparkled the air beneath the smiling sun;
The birdlings made their love on every side;
Ouvrière and ouvrier pass'd hand in hand;
Pass'd gaily mounted squire and amazone;
Armorial bearings deck'd rich chariots;
Pha'ton, plain cabriolet, a countless throng,
Mounted, descended from the arch of stars;
And, yes, a noce, and fair the youthful bride.
All nature smiling, nature's chiefest work,
All men, smil'd back again, attun'd
To all the joyous influence of the time.
Yet, in the music, as a minor tone,
Almost is borne a sigh upon the breeze;
Beside the fountain, 'neath the flowering trees,
Each sat, in joyous summer, sad and lone.

II.

We hasten'd, when the trees were black and bare
Past fountains silent, ice-bound, dark and drear.
No passers greeting gave, silent they hurry on,
Each one wrapt selfishly in anxious thought;
Deserted the long vistas of bare trees,
Save by some gendarme muffled in his cape;
Upward, toward the arch, along the slipp'ry road
A gibbet drag, creaking beneath the weight
Chain'd underneath it of a block of stone
Like a sarcophagus, toils slow and sad;
Day fading gloomily; unlit the lamps;
One poor dead frozen sparrow by the path
To tell his comrades dead or flown afar;
All nature chill'd and desolate and sad
Speaking no cheerful words to human hearts;
Yet, clinging each to each, and hastening on,
By ice-bound fount, 'neath branches black and bare,
We turn and smile to-day. Ah! neither is alone.

THE BEST PART OF LIFE.

(From Alessandro da Vamora.)

I.

Acolto :

I read the poems of those to whom sad fate
Denied love's sweet caresses. What the word,
Wise, patient, scornful, full of faith and prayer,
Alike to me a bitterness of wrong,
A cry of victims stainèd every song.
[Stainèd alike victim of unfair self,
Man's love of fairest things, man's love of pelf,
Prudence, advantage for a life-long stay,
All things that love usurp, deprive to-day
Lovers of love's fruition, seek a morrow
May come, may not, still leave to-day a sorrow.]

II.

Speralto :

I read the poems of love. The lovers sang :
That when beside the loved one, cold nor heat
Nor storms, nor bare surroundings, scarce were known.
Riches and honor, praise or friends, were less
Than presence of the loved one, love's caress.
[If love's life's best, and we can live but once,
Sad is the life that ends and knows not love.
I joy, and you. They grieve that we may joy?
Is there no better way, no way without alloy?
Praise for each way that blesses, praise alway.
Oh! might its sorrows pass, its blessings stay.]

PRACTICALITY.

[A DIPTYCH.]

I.

You who, in the parks, through the sultry nights,
Seated or pacing bear your pallid babes,
You, mothers, you who all these thirty years
Scarce for one hour have been absent from my thoughts,
That it is thirty years, forgive. Bear not
Your wrongs, your griefs, your sufferings, before
The tribunal of justice, earth's or heaven's.
Plead not my lagging, if others have outrun.
Veil your accusing eyes, nor bid them shame
A wavering hand, dull brain, and eye so dim,
Help, if perceived, ill sped, sped not at all.
Yours be the mercy we have lack'd. Plead not
Our slow brought help or our indifference.
Count not your dead, count not the days and nights
In stifling homes returning year by year.
Our blundering past, poor present, future—all forgive.

II.

But you fair darlings of all happiest homes,
Bred in sweet airs and gentlest gales of heaven,
Nurtured with all that life can give of joy,
Plead you before the tribunal of love.
Plead by your beauty, you whom health makes fair,
Plead with your mothers, all that love you. Leave
No heart untouch'd, no brain or hand unmoved,
Till all are seeking, finding, pressing on,
Find them or build them homes as sane as yours.
Let, who build aught, build wiser or as wise,
Who build not, claim the best of them who build,
Till fault by fault, faults bred through man's device,
By man's device be conquered, put away;
So from life's canvas fade, mother and pallid babe,
To be but as a dream, a weary dream that's past—
Through joy 'tis far away alone a memory.

NEEDLESS LOSSES.

I.

When on my house top, far away from care,
Over the tree tops, soft the summer air
Comes wafted, where the broad roof shadows me,
My flow'rs about me, some for humming-birds,
Thistles for yellow-hammers, thyme for bees,
Sweet perfumed flowers for the one I love,
I think me of the old and sick and poor,—
You, poet, in the house on street confined,
Losing the summer wind, the night of stars, —
You hunchback, bedrid in your tenement,—
You, brother of singers, palsied on your bed,—
Knowing your wretched fellows myriad,
Seeing, through habit, such sweet gifts shut out,
I sigh, half thinking every effort vain
Would mind men not to lose as well as gain.

II.

Then when I think of you too, Ivan brave,
Drear decades faithful to your agèd dam,
You, poor old Constant, by the closèd gate,
You, Sylvan, with your hopeless dreams of joy,
You Cherdos, you Cavarodel,
And all your kind (endless as stars,
As stars as pure, as single shining on,)
Wearing out life in vainest sacrifice,
Vainest, since needless, (like the dazèd stag's,
Stopped by a slender thread across his path,)
As walls material that needless shut out joy
Seem customs, laws, contrivances of men
That, seeming needful, needless shut out joy,
Make many gain, make you, dear brothers, lose.

(From Allessandro da Vermora.)

DRIFTING.

[A LEAF OF A DIPTYCH.]

I succored more than I will tell,
I trusted utterly for love,
Was uséd to the fill, the while
Who uséd, careful or careless cut
The cords that bound me to my best.
I drifted forth, and 'woke to find
My cable parted, compass and rudder gone,
And all I trusted, I alone and ill.
I who had built my ship, and made
It worth one's while to voyage with me,
Shall I construct again, when faith is dead;
 Or shall I drift, and drift,
 And so drift out to sea
 Afar from God and thee,
 Drift out into the night,
A night that knows no morrow ?
Ah ! if surcease of sorrow
 That night bring to my heart,
 So best that we should part,
  And I should be
   Adrift
  And drifting out to sea.

ONE BREATH OF INDIAN SUMMER.

[A LEAF OF A DIPTYCH.]

I dreamed that one estranged, one once too loved,
Was near me, but with face averted as of wont for long.
I, and not he, on that estrangement stood.   He gave the cause.
And yet, both in my dream, and when I waked, all day,
A pleasant sense was with me of his nearness, kin to love ;
And even with face averted, his as mine,
Near me he seemed still dear.   Ah ! why ?
Him I had loved had never been ;
His form had housed unworthiness,
So nought to me.   I knew it, yet I once had thought
That in that house I held a friend.
[Ah, but dear friends, this past is one
Can never be explained away ;
I was mistaken as to what the house contained ;
Its owners changed not ; they remained the same ;
Unworthy of a good man's love from first to last.]
I ne'er had loved the house except for what
It had contained, but in my cheated thought ;
Itself was not so fair that I should love it, save for those within;
They never were within it I had fancied there and loved ;
And yet, when near that house, but in a dream, a moment's space
Old love came back, or present love, ne'er changed or dead,
But only curtained off from sight, so passed for gone,
Or love, new born perhaps, born in my dream,
Came tender from the skies to me returning,
Is with me now, has been with me all day,   [come back,
And breathes an atmosphere of Indian summer's summer days
Of love impossible made possible,
Of ineffaceable effaced,
Of changeless changed and wrong made right,
That still stays by me all this Indian summer day.

IN THE TREASURY.

[The Just Worshipper:—What you doubt I affirm not.]

The Queen of Sheba gave great Solomon
A parting gift surpassing all the rest;
Two precious jars, rich jewelled, each one filled
With dust mysterious of the elder world,
Wherein the echoes of his wisdom fell,
To sleep there potent for all time to come.
Minutest portion of the one cast forth
Toward coming pestilence would drive it back;
The other had like power o'er spirits dire,
Could drive them back and shut the gates of hell.

These, as the richest treasures of his crown,
Sol'mon did guard. But in his happy reign,
Made safe by wisdom, scarce or pestilence
Or spirits dire e'er asked their use. More late,
If used howe'er, their store still wasted not.

When came the taking of Jerusalem,
These jars were captive borne to Babylon,
And when the Jews returnèd home, held back;
And, aye since handed down from power to power,
Are held this day by one small Eastern tribe,
Poor, weak, half taught, and rich in only this.

These jars, the keen thrift of our modern times,
For this our Western world would now acquire,

To drive back peril from her cities fair,
Threatened of pestilence and spirits dire.

You mock at spirits? at the tale yet more?
Find it but clumsy? call it newly made?
Proved old the tale, doubt still the jars exist?
If shown the jars, doubt they were Solomon's?
Or proved the jars came straight from Solomon,
Doubt if he e'er believed they held such power?
Doubt, last, that they, whate'er wise Sol'mon thought,
Hold or have ever held the power they claim;
And failing this, what boots it all the rest
Be true or false? Idle the storied links
Or chain complete that drags a worthless gift;
Its worth not provable, the rest is idly proved;
Proved this, the rest may follow or may not,
Ours still their power o'er pestilence and hell.

Paling the glory of King Solomon,
With light more heavenly fair, a teacher comes;
Wisdom, if his, is wisdom, whether sprung
From elder wisdom or from lips divine.
If his the wisdom that hath power to make
Men whole and clean, and shut out every harm,
That power remains, though doubt surround the tale
Of birth or miracle or cruel death;
Is ours forever, if his truth be truth,
His gift accordant with the needs of men,
His laws harmonious with eternal law;
Can bless us still. A righteous life our aim,
Can make us fit for Heaven, be there one,
Make earth a heaven, be there other none.
The end of all devotion's love and ruth,
Bring in—the reign of Righteousness and Truth.

WORDS FOR ILLUMINATIONS, OR TO ACCOMPANY ILLUSTRATIONS.

TOWER OF IVORY!

[For a richly illuminated page, addressed to one who criticised the poet's handwriting, and showing,—beneath a crest, and above the flowers named in the poem, shown as prone before it—the initial letter of a Lady's name, formed by the name being written thrice across the page, twice parallel and once athwart; the letters of the name (showing as capitals) illuminated in gold and the colors of the flowers, and each letter also serving in its appropriate place in the text.]

THE CIRCLING YEAR.

[Written to accompany the gift of a book of views of twelve capitals of columns carved with designs illustrative of the progress of the year : icicles, bare branches, budding boughs, early leafage, full foliage, flowers, fruit, and evergreens, and with birds mating, nest-building, feeding their young, teaching them to fly, and flying southward.]

THE SONG OF THE ROSE.

[For an illumination in which, upon a golden trellis, in verdant text, as if foliage, and budding sometimes into tenderer tints as if into buds and flowers, is seen to cling the Song, like a climbing rose.]

THE CLIMBING ROSE.

[L'envoy, written under the Song of the Rose.]

A TEMPLE PORCH.

WITH A JEWELLED " DAMOISELLE."

AN IRIS.

A PORTRAIT.

A TIME SERENE.

BENEDICTUS QUI PATITUR.

OH, tower of ivory, all the silent night
I watched the splendid cereus unfold
PetAl by petal ⊢ill its wealth of bloom
With beauty seemed to fill the crystal dome.
No lady, thRough the whole wide world save one,
Could fitly image forth that royal flower,
In beauty like thⱲ wondRous orient queen
That shone on Sol'mon and his glory paled.
But, when the morn—ng broke startlǀng the watchers
And sent its violet rays athwart our fading lamps.
And nature smiled radiant and elatE,
THe morning's gloℛy seemed her fittest flower.
The budding morn swift blossomed inTo day,
And in A garden all of roses one arose
Perfectest mid peℛfection, loveliest, best.
Bearing in peRfumed breast a crystal tear
Of tender pity for ◀ world less fair.
Who bears the ceRens and the morning's flower.
Pitying the griefs sⲒe is too fair to share,
Be hers, O rose, since earlǀest time the queen
And type of every loveliest flower that blows.
Lady, here at your feet I lay thEm all,
Prone as the phantom sheaves of Joseph's dream.
My task is done, and proved my wriTing fair.
For see, her name all fairest bars the page,
Shielding my vagrant lines from your disdain.

WHEN icy-laden branches bending low,
But image forth my heart—its stifled flow—
 Its chilled faith—its doubt of good,
 Of endless bliss, of living word—
  Once by your side,
  All these to blot
 Your presence has the wondrous power,
 And gives to me a smiling hour,
 With all my doubts and cares forgot.

When February boughs are bare,
And faith is dead, and only care
 And doubt are mine—
  Once by your side,
  Ne'er I repine—
In the sweet summer of your smile,
Summer and faith return awhile.

When erst dead boughs with budding life are swelling,
And smiling skies to waking earth are telling
 That spring is come—and yet I cry,
  Not unto me!
  Once by your side—
Within my heart the birds are carolling,
 And smiles the sky,
 I know not why—
I only know it is when you are by.

When summer's fruits o'erlap its flowers,
And glow for me life's dearest hours,
And only sweetest cares I bear,
Yet almost doubt if I am blest,
Thus longing with a vague unrest—
  Once by your side,
  No doubts beguile—
All hours are brighter for your smile.

Ah ! when, like summer days, for me
You cease to smile, where shall I be ?
　　　What be my lot ?
　　　Unblest and drear
　　　Where you are not.
　　Fallen my fruit, my foliage sere,
And sunward flown the swallow dear,
　　Gifted with such a gracious power,
To make sweet Summer of my wintriest hour.

Sunward flown ! ah ! who can know
If we shall be : or being, woe
Or weal be ours ! When all, alas !
Of life's sweet summer hours shall pass,
Of what avail shall Christmas boughs
Adorn for us December's brows ?
Ah ! who shall tell ! I know but this,
　　　Once by your side
　　　All life is bliss,
Parted I doubt of all but pain,
Till you bring summer back to me again.

THE SONG OF THE ROSE.

Forth shone the Sun in his splendour,
 Red glowed the Rose in his sight ;
Fair lay the garden around it,
 Glittering with flowerets so bright
That the Rose stood unnoticed among them ;
But in light and in being rejoicing,
 It sung in its heart but one song :
Me, too, hath nature made beautiful,
 Made without power of wrong ;
  I all completeness am,
  I am all sweetness—ah !
  Take me and lay me, sweet,
 A sweet in thy sweeter breast.
Take me full blown, all completeness,
 Full blown, but ah ! not o'er blown yet ;
A chalice full freighted with sweetness,
 With colour and perfume unflown yet.
But the days they are passing, are passing ;
 One by one soon my petals must fall,
Then take them and lay them, sweet,
Sweets in thy sweeter breast,
 Now whilst thou may'st take them all.

Why wait'st thou, my love, oh ! my goddess,
 Take thine own, as thine own give me rest ;
Ere the days that are passing have passed, love,
 Lay love in thy lov'lier breast—
[Not a rose but a passion-flower would'st thou ?
 Then farewell—no, not so—give me rest ;
Lay the rose in the passion-flower's place, love,
 And 'twill turn to one there when 'tis prest.]

TO THE CLIMBING ROSE.

CLIMB, oh! climb the golden lattice,
    Song of mine;
Climb 'till thou dost reach her heart,
    For whom I pine.

Cease not, lest thou lose the bliss
    For which I sigh;
Climb 'till thou dost touch her heart!
    Ah! why not I?

SONNET.

[With a promised gift of a picture in which a church porch is seen bridging a stream]

How shall I ever cross, dear love,
  The river cold of your indifference ?
    How find, to give me rest at last,
    As in a quiet haven when the storms are past,
  From doubts asylum, and from fears a safe defense,
In the pure temple of your sheltering love ?
    O, worshipped long, the temple must
      Throw me it's porch across the stream,
    Yielding its portal's keys, for sacred trust,
      To one it leads from earth to heaven.
    Asylum, sweeter than a heavenly dream,
      True Salem, to thy worshipper given !
Build thou the porch through which love's pathway lies,
And bridge my entrance into paradise.

THE IRIS.

O flower that draws me to the water side,
   Stain'd with rich purple as the robe of kings ;
Yet a poor humble flow'r that ne'er the poet sings
   Beside the lily and the eglantine ;
   No rose, no queen of flowers, yet all mine,
     Stain'd as my thought with purple fit for kings ;
     Flow'r half despised, unnoted, all unsung,
   Set stiff upon thy stalk, not lightly bending,
   But bent, quick broke ; once broken, broke for aye,
   Yet with a sad vitality that lives,
   Blooms on, so broken, blooms, but faded too :
Fading all swiftly if not nourish'd as thy wont,—
   Thy wont, or need—all thy thirst met ;
Coarse flow'r, and strong ; frail flow'r, whose petal lightly tears ;
     Gilded within ; symbol of trinities ;
     Gifted with sweetness to despisers lost :
     Mystic, rich, poor, despis'd, dear flow'r ;
     Symbol of me, half strong, all weak :
   Thy place (then blest) beside cool waters pure ;
     Yet, since acceptant, blooming oft in dust ;
   Ill found along the highway, out of place :
     Half blooming there ; not knowing well thy place ;
     Ill choosing, smiling, torn, forgot !

A PORTRAIT.

[To an invalid lady who had received a madonna lily,
champney roses, heliotrope and orchids.]

Who, with the spotless lily called
  For her heaven named blessedest,
  Laid blushing roses, love's own flower,
  But with a blush as fair as spake
  A love most gentle, tender, pure ;
  And with them laid blooms sweet as are
  The gracious actions of a gracious life ;
  Then sought a rare and tropic flower
  Of prizèd race and nature delicate ;
  Then all encinctured with a band as green
  As are the memories of good men's lives—
Gave trifling solace to sad pain tried hours,
But painted her to whom he gave the flowers.

A TIME SERENE.

In younger and less quiet days,
The autumn leaves I loved did blaze
With red : my life was but a maze,
With flashing lights along its ways.

But now, I hear the name, Irene,
And 'tis the yellow leaf whose sheen
I love : my life a path serene,
With shade, where sunlight lies between.

BENEDICTUS QUI PATITUR.

Passing at midnight down the little tangled stair,
My lamp light falling soft on blazons there
　　Where hung the armories the children loved,
　　I smiled to think the tales they held with me.
　　Half held for truth, still held for their nobility.
　　And graver smiled chancing these words to see :
　　　　Benedictus qui patitur.

Sable the antient shield, and borne thereon thrice pied,
Twin plumes of argent, ech'llon set, or tied ;
　　Above, for crest, the helm of one who served
　　The Holy Roman Empire long, a faithful knight,
　　'Neath crowns plumed argent sable as for day and night.
　　And underneath this legend fit bedight :
　　,　　Benedictus qui patitur.

Godfroid the Count von Benedict, if stories stand,
This bore on 's shield into the Holy Land,
　　Leaving behind the wife and child he loved,
　　And when the close of one long hard fought day
　　Saw cross o'erborne and death struck Godfroid lay,
　　He smiled, and on these words he sighed his soul away:
　　　　Benedictus qui patitur.

The golden lilies of the kings of France are borne
Upon a field of stainless white.　Foresworn
　　Or pure their souls ! who knows the soul?
　　When the dread night of St. Bartholemew was o'er
　　Homeless they sought asylum on a stranger shore,
　　Who fain would keep the faith their fathers held of yore.
　　　　Benedictus qui patitur.

And when the prelate and the crown combined
In after years to curb their souls, behind
    They left th'asylum for a wilderness;
Across the sea with single hearts they fared,
Hunger and thirst and savage foe they dared,
Cold and disease. Few lived ; we spring from those were spared.
    Benedictus qui patitur.

The night wind through the casement where the roses swing
Stirs soft, and waves my lamp light as one questioning ;
    I know my children sleep as safe to night,
As ne'er were paynim, zealot, priest nor king.
We suffer not.   Has then the blessing too ta'en wing ?
Scarce dare I sigh what some were wont to sing :
    Benedictus qui patitur.

Shapes of the past that with the night have come,
Find ye me recreant ? People ye my home !
    Raise in our hearts the standard of the past.
Not for the faith that best could bring them ease.
Respect, men's smiles, our fathers suffered. What heaven please
So let me hold.   Mine be the truth that conscience sees.
    Benedictus qui patitur.

FOUR SCHOOL AND COLLEGE SONGS.

I. Boating Song.   III. The Two Bob-o'-links.
II. Far-off Friends.   IV. Kineherd's Song.

Boating Song.

Come comrades sing a joyous song,
As o'er the waves we bound along ;
      Our voices chime,
      Our oars keep time,
   Our hearts are light and free.

We'll sing, we'll sing a joyous song, etc.

And as we skim the waters o'er,
   As we skim the waters o'er,
Fainter and fainter grows the shore,
   Fainter grows the shore.

            Keep time,
               Keep time.
            Keep time,
               Keep time,

Keep time, keep time, the evening star
Lights up her silver lamp afar ;
      Her tender ray
      Succeeds the day
   And calls to rest and love.

The evening star, the evening star, etc.

Yet still we sing our joyous song,
And o'er the waves we bound along,
      While voices chime,
      And oars keep time,
   And hearts are light and free.

Together, together we bend upon our oars.
Together, together we bend upon our oars.

FAR-OFF FRIENDS.

When the hours of day are past
 And my work is laid aside,
Oft I watch a fading west
 Late with purple dyed.
  And I ask : Where can they be?
  And I wonder wistfully,
   Wonder, wonder wistfully,
    Wond'ring ever,
    Asking never,
  Do they ever think of me.

Often in the silent night,
 When the house is wrapped in sleep,
I look out across the dark,
 Shoreward o'er the deep.
  And I ask : Where can they be?
  And I wonder wistfully
   Wonder, wonder wistfully
    Wond'ring ever
    Asking never
  Do they ever think of me.

THE TWO BOB-O'-LINKS.

In the bright summer sunshine I love to be singing,
  Singing, singing, for I'm Bob-o'-lincoln ;
With music and laughter I keep the fields ringing,
  Ringing, ringing, for I'm Bob-o'-link.
        I hear someone calling.
          Madame? Good morning.
        What news have you for me?
              Ah! . . . Ha ha! ha ha!
Ha ha ha, ha ha! I love to be jolly,
  Jolly, jolly, for I'm Bob-o'-lincoln.
To sigh and lament and complain, oh, what folly!
  I always keep laughing, I, Bob-o'-link,

              Bob-o'-link,
                Bob-o'-link,
                  Bob-o'-lincoln.

O, my heart with gladness is bubbling over,
  Bubbling over, bubbling over, bubbling over, bubbling over
I do no work and yet live I in clover,
  I live in clover, I live in clover, live in clover, in clover.

And through the long hour when the reapers are nooning,
  Nooning, nooning, and taking their drink,
I swing on the grain and my pipes I keep tuning,
  Tuning, tuning, for—I'm Bob-o'-link.
        Bob-o'-lincoln, bob'-lincoln,
          Ha ha! Bob'-lincoln!

            Oh what gladness,
            Banishing sadness,
            Banishing sadness
              Ever away!

          Away, away, away!
            Ou lu lu la,
              Ou lu lu,
              Away,
                Ha ha!
Ou lu lu, lu lu, lu lu la! lu lu la, lu lu, . . . lulu   lu
  . . . lu. . . .

THE PYRENEAN KINE-HERD.

Come home my lowing herd,
  Come home, my kine, come home with me.
The sun is swiftly sinking
    To his home beyond the sea,
      The birds have all ceased their singing,
        We must no longer roam ;
          The bees have hush'd their humming,
            For soon the night is coming.
Come home, my lowing herd,
  Come home, my kine, come home.

Haste! Hoy! the storm is coming,
  And the moor, and the moor, is drear and lone ;
I see the lightning flashing
    And I hear, and I hear, the thunder tone.
      Haste, ere the swollen torrent
        Sweeps the worn bridge away.
          Oh, the night is dark and dreary,
            And my feet, my feet, are weary ;—
But the lights of home now I see !
  There my loved ones wait for me.
O, the lights of home now I see,
  Where my lassie waits for me.
    Come home my lowing herd,
      Come home, my kine, with me.
        Come home,
          Come home.

FOUR MINSTREL SONGS.

MOLLY TRUE.

. Verses written in 1861.

Away down South whar de live oaks wave,
   Whar de sun shines bright, an' de cane brakes grow,
A river flows upon whose waves
   I used to love my boat to row.
     An' dar de waves dey sing to me
      De sweetest song I ever knew :
     Molly loves, she loves you well,
      She loves you dearly, loves you true.

Yes, Molly love' dis nigger well,
   She love' me dearly, love' me true,
An' oder darkies when dey see her,
   Wish dey had a Molly too.
     Her eyes were like de summer night,
      Or stars dat shine in heaven's clear blue.
     An' den her smile ! It seemed to say
      Your Molly loves you, loves you true.

One evenin', when de sun was low,
   I lay me down and shut my eye,
An' den I dreamp' a dreadful dream
   I'll ne'er forget until I die.
     I dreamp' dey stole my love away,
      An' whar she gone I never knew,
     An', in the morning when I wake,
      Dey tole me dat my dream was true.

O yes, I lov'd my Molly well,
   I lov'd her dearly, lov'd her true,
An' somfing seems to whisper me
   Dat Molly lov'd her Sambo too.
     And, when at night de moon ride high,
      And all are wrapped in sleep but me,
     I tink I hear an angel's voice.
     It is my Molly calling me.

[Verse added in 1865.]

De morning breaks, de sun shine bright,
   De night of wrong and chains is past.
I heer de happy people say :
   De black men all are free at last.
     But tho' the right to wrong be dead,
      Behind de wound de scars remain.
     Dey can to Sambo freedom give,—
      But not his Molly back again.

ELEGY.

[WORDS FOR MUSIC.]

I.

Down in the valley he is sleeping,
  There where the wild flowers gently wave,
Where sighing pines their watch are keeping,
  He sleeps the slumber of the brave.

    Sweetly the oriole above him,
        Above him, above him,
    Echoes their sighs who long will love him,
        Whom they shall see no more,

            No more!

        Glow crimson east, with blush of morning,
          Glow summer days above his grave,
        Glow golden west, his couch adorning
          Who sleeps the slumber of the brave.

II.

Brave are the hearts which are most tender,
  Tender the hearts which are most brave,
Faithful the lives which life surrender,
  Losing the bliss they die to save.

Soft fell the dews of night above him,
  Above him, above him,
Warm fall their tears who long will love him,
  Whom they shall see no more.

No more !

Glow crimson east with blush of morning,
  Glow summer days above his grave,
Glow golden west his couch adorning,
  Who sleeps the slumber of the brave.

Soft breathe the winds there in the southland,
  Laden'd with fragrance of wild bay,
Spicy with breath of Indian roses,
  Whispering above him night and day.

He sleeps
Where the same stars look down :
He sleeps,
Sleeps.

MARY FAR AWAY.

[WORDS FOR MUSIC.]

Shall I ever see again thy sweet presence Mary,
　Shall I ever hear the voice so dear to me,
Shall I ever stroke again thy tresses, little fairy,
　While these longing arms enfold my Mary?

Often, in the silent night, in dreams I see my Mary,
　O, she seems an angel bright, yet dear to me,
Soft I feel upon my cheek the breathing of a fairy,
　Lo, these arms enfold at last, my Mary.

But the morning breaks at last, flown are dreams of Mary
　Far, oh far, away that form so dear to me
Then I kneel and pray for blessings, blessings on my Mary,
　All good angels guard and bless and bring me back my Mary,
　All good angels guard and bless and bring me back my Mary.

　　O my love, Mary dear to me,
　　　Come back love to me, Mary dear to me,
　　O my love, Mary dear to me,
　　　O, come back, my darling Mary.

BEYOND THE STARS.

[Words for Music.]

I shall never see again thy sweet presence, Mary,
  I shall never hear the voice so dear to me;
Where they laid that gentle form Oh! the shore is lonely;
  Only there the sweet sad waves answering endlessly:

        Far away,
        Far away,
    Mary's far away beyond the stars,
      Far beyond the stars.

  I shall never see her form again,
    I shall never hear her tender voice.
Never in these longing arms fold my gentle fairy,
  Nevermore, nevermore. Oh! my darling Mary!

But the silent night brings still ofttimes dreams of Mary,
  I am waiting by the shore for her I love;
Lo! afar the nearing sail brings my little fairy.
  Tenderly, O stately ship bear my love to me.

        Far away,
        Far away,
    Mary's far away beyond the stars,
      Far beyond the stars.

  Vainly I call that name so dear to me,
    Vainly stretch out my arms for that dear form.
" Mary dwells with angels now " someone whispers weeping,
" Far away, far away, far away beyond the stars."

SERENADES AND MISCELLANEOUS SONGS.

My Star.

Star of my soul, when night rides in the firmament
And countless orbs the harmonies of law proclaim,
Deep in my soul they wake an answering harmony,
They wake the answering harmony of thy dear name.

Each silent sphere its course appointed circling
Signals its fellows still.
So, when the night of doubt and wrong
Broods o'er my soul, what wakes my song?
Changeless and pure, serene, afar
Dawns thy pure light, my star, my star,
Changeless and pure, serene, afar
Dawns bright my soul's sweet lamp, my star, my star.

My guiding star!
And when the clouds of doubt and sorrow multiply
She will not leave me,
E'en though through fault or fate I may not to her fly,
Ah, may not wing across the sky
To that sweet rest.

I know that she will fail me not e'en though all else should fail.
Though voids as trackless as the sky
My path divide from hers for aye,
Changeless and pure, serene, afar
Shines on for me my guiding star,
Steadfast, undimm'd, all pure afar
Burns bright my soul's sweet lamp, my star, my star.

SERENADE.

Softly the night winds come
Through the dark wood creeping,
And tender stars look down
Whilst thou, my love, art sleeping.
All nature slumbers,
Rests from its weary day's labour.
Only my heart,
The weary hours numbers;
Only my heart,
Watches and longs for thee.

And as the night winds come
Fanning thy slumber,
And from thy soft cheeks snatch
Soft kisses without number.
I would be night wind,
Night wind blown no man knows whither,
If once, but once,
My wings would bear me thither,
Bear me but once
To snatch a kiss from thee.

Lo ! now the rising wind
All the wood is shaking,
Wak'st thou not, my love ?
Oh ! wake, my heart is breaking ;
I'll ne'er forsake thee,
Then if not storm, oh, let love awake thee ;
Oh, wake and say
My heart may rest on thine, love ;
Say my worn heart
May rest at last on thine.

SERENADE.

THE stilly night, the whispering wind,
   The shadows weird beneath the trees ;
The waning moon, the drifting cloud,
   The fitful perfume on the breeze ;
My weary heart that knows no rest
   'Till thou dost come, all call to thee.
   Oh ! come, my life, my love, to me,
And clasp me fainting on thy breast.

The night will pass, the wind will die,
   The shadows with the moon depart ;
The perfume fade, the hour pass by
   When thou canst clasp me on thine heart.
But I shall changeless pine 'till pressed
   Once in thine arms of circling snow,
   Oh ! come, and never let me go,
So I may be forever blest.

MELODY.

When the silent night returns,
And the lamp of Venus burns,
Soft above the olive grove
Comes the hour of silent love.
    Nearer, nearer, not a word,
    Love's sweet voice is felt, not heard ;
    Smile, oh tender stars above !
    Hail, dear hour of silent love !

When I raised my eyes to thine,
Only trusting love in mine ;
Thine but said, oh ! love, to me,
Nearer, nearer let us be.
    Nearer, nearer let us be,
    Drifting barks on perfumed sea,
    While the stars smile soft above
    On the hour of silent love.

When thine eye so soft and clear,
Filled with passion's tender tear,
Dropped its sweetness into mine,
Then I knew that I was thine.
    Nearer, nearer, not a sound,
    Enter on enchanted ground,
    While the stars smile soft above
    On an hour of silent love.

IN SPRING TIME.

I wandered in the springtime
All down a flowery lane,
Soft airs blew off the lilac's breath,
Then blew it back again :
Ah ! such another springtime
Will never come again.

The bobolink's soft fluting
Rose liquid from the grass ;
The air was filled with gladness—
Captious, I cried, Alas !
Sure such another springtime
Will never come to pass.

Arbutus flowers, creeping
Beneath the chestnut wood,
Whispered their love in secret,
And whispered Love is good ;
Such days return, ah ! never,
Alas, I wish they would.

The bull frog piped melodious,
The cricket's chirp was bliss ;
What could the reason be, who knows ?
I only know but this :
That day I learned, O day of days !
The sweetness of a kiss.

[Verses resulting from treating a melody contrapuntally, and then following the indications of the music in words, which in turn create a legend, for which an appropriate date is then found.]

SHAMUS MORIATY;

OR,

THE BELLS OF ST. HILLARY.

[An incident of the rebellion of 1798.]

Brave rang out the bells of Saint Hillary,
Rang the tune puts a man in the pillory,—
    Erin go bragh
    Sounded afar.
O that swate darlin' tune, Erin go bragh!

It rang, and rang, and waked up the peasantry.
Who dare ring that tune for a pleasantry?
    Erin go bragh!
    Troth, don't ye knaw
His life's in danger, rings *Erin go bragh?*

Came the squire and swate Misthress Milligan,
Came his Riv'rance Father O'Killigan,
    Quick came they all,
    Great folk and small,
Drawn by the music of *Erin go bragh.*

The hunters' horns now took up the melody,
Bay'd the hounds as if scintin' a felony:
    Men hang to-day,
    Not far away,
For less than for ringin' out Erin go bragh.

O, 'twas fine. But woe to swate Shamus now!
" Shamus, Shamus, come from that belfry-mow,"
    Call'd now the neighbors all,
    Came his swate mother's call,
Minglin' with hers that he loved best of all.

" Come down, come down, ye madcap, the bailiff's men
Here'll be straight.   Ye'll find to yer sorrow then
     Ye'll rue the day
     Ye dared to play
On those damned bells blessed *Erin go bragh.*"

Shamus, Shamus, up in the belfry tall,
Niver, niver heeded their words at all.
     Far and away,
     Rang out that day,
That tune the Saxon hates: *Erin go bragh.*

" Oh ! boy, the bailiff's men come !   And the soldiery,
Out the town gate !   Och, soldiers wid musketry !
     Troth, don't ye hear ?
     Sure they're close here !
They're nigh at the tower door ! Yer lost, Shamus dear !"

No, not yet.   He swings from the belfry tall,
Down the ivy, over the churchyard wall ;
     Far and away,
     Shamus that day
Flew, like the wind, shoutin' *Erin go bragh.*

He flies, 'mid cries : " The hounds, are they after him ? "
" No, not yet, the saints are protectin' him."
     " Erin go bragh "
     He shouts back from afar,
" Ireland forever, and *Erin go bragh !* "

But see ! the hounds ! Good God, they are on his track !
Call them off.   Too late !   They are at his back.
     A shot ?   From the town !
     Oh, Shamus goes down,
Shot, torn by dogs, cryin' *Erin go bragh.*

" Whip them off.   Oh, sure he is breathin' still."
" No.   He'll breathe niver more now, do what ye will."
     Torn, yet so fair,
     Poor Shamus lies there,
Dead, for a tune !   His dirge : *Erin go bragh.*

O, sweet Shandon, green be yer flow'ry meads,
Gently flow yer waters; of gallant deeds
      Whisper ye low,
      Where'er ye flow.
Forget not how Shamus rang *Erin go bragh.*

Oh! Shamus boy, my sad tears are fallin' whin
E'er thy brave sad fate I'm recallin' thin,
      Shamus mavourneen,
      Shamus asthore,
Savourneen deelish! Och, cregan oh!

Swate echoes, 'round that old belfry stealin'
Sound ofttimes like bells softly pealin'
      And, by that shore,
      Now evermore,
Hovers the music of *Erin go bragh.*

Loud ring out, ye bells, from yer clatter-mow,
Ring what tunes ye may,—'tis no matter now;
      Erin go bragh,
      Erin go bragh,
Whate'er yer tune, we hear *Erin go bragh.*

Ring loud, ring soft, ye bells, but ye ever will
Ring a dirge to Shamus, his last words still:
      " *Erin go bragh,*
      Erin go bragh,
Ireland for ever, and *Erin go bragh.*"

When the one I love is near me
  Never vexings come me near,
Never care, nor ever sorrow ;
  Far is question, doubt, and fear.
    'Verdant then the fields, tho' winter ;
    Birdlings carol ; all things sweetly
    Chaunt the endless hymn of nature,
When the one I love is near me,
  When the one I love is near.

SHOULD'ST THOU STAND ON THE GOLDEN STAIR.

Should'st thou stand on the golden stair
    Of Heaven's high battlement,
And from that starry height look down
      On thy past self afar,
    Think'st thou that ne'er one pitying thrill
    Athwart the joy of pardon still
        Would steal?
      Who made thee gave each longing sweet,
      Each joy and doubt and fear.
        In yielding, or in thwarting, wrong?
        For which is pardon giv'n?

FIVE DEVOTIONAL PIECES.

Cradle Song.

Sleep my baby, sweetly sleep,
Thy mother watch will o'er thee keep,
  Bending o'er the little bed
  Pillowing thy tiny head.

   Care and trouble, though they come,
   Though thou wand'rest far from home,
     Thy mother's heart, I still will keep
     A mother's heart. Sleep, baby, sleep.

Sleep my baby. While the throng
Of angels hymn for aye their song
  Before Him, still one angel keeps
  Watch where my little baby sleeps.

   Oh! my heart, be still, be still.
   Whate'er comes will be His will.
     Sleep my baby, while I keep
     My mother watch. Sleep, baby, sleep.

A RANTER'S HYMN.

Wide o'er all the grave yards
 Sounds the trump of doom.
  All must rise ;
  Some to the skies,
 Some sink to gloom.
   Dreadful Judge Eternal,
    Grant me that I may
     Find in thee
     Security,
    Ere that awful day,

Ere that day of mourning,
 Ere that day of woe.
  O that sorrow
  No to-morrow
 E'er shall know.
   Who shall stand before him
    When the Judge shall sit,
     And what's been
     Well hid 's seen,
    All in dooms-book writ,

All the mean excuses.
 All the lies and feints ?
  Excuses lame
  Won't hide their shame,
 It blacker paints.
   Hell gapes full of torment
    For the sinner then,
     And the fire
     Mounting higher
    Hastes to feed on men,

Feed and feed forever,
  Never burn them up.
    The trumpet sounds,
    And all on hounds
  To drink their cup,
        Drink the cup of fire ;
          And the burning lake
            Spreads out wide
            On every side.
          Not one shall escape.

The eleventh hour soundeth,
  'Tis not yet too late.
    That hour is past.
    Now sounds the last
  Dread hour of fate.
        O'er all the graves it soundeth,
          The midnight of the world,
            And God forsaken
            All must waken
            And to hell be hurled.

———

High o'er all this anguish,
  Hymning joyous songs,
    Redeemed choirs
    Strike their lyres
  In countless throngs.
      These are they have washéd
        Their robes the Lamb's blood in,
          And there on high
          Will sing for aye,
        Cleanséd from all sin :

To the King eternal,
  To the Son Divine,
    To the Dove
    That broods in love,
  Supernal Trine,
      Endless, endless praises
        Sound along the shore
          Of thy sea,
          Eternity,
        Now and evermore.

          ———

Now and evermore,
  O, now and ever more !
    Can I bear
    That not to share,
  That sweet high joy ?
      Take me, friend of sinners,
        Cleanse me from my sin,
          And let be
          My part with thee
        Evermore. Amen.

THE ADORATION OF THE MAGI.

[A Jesu-worshipper's Hymn at the season of the Epiphany.]

The gentiles shall come to thy light, and Kings to the brightness of thy rising.   Isaiah xl : 5

And behold there came wise men, saying : we have seen his star in the east and have come to worship him . . . . and they presented unto him gifts, gold, frankincense and myrrh.   Matt. ii : 11.

A strain of strange and sad, but sweet music ; then follows the hymn.

Wise, from afar, I come,
Following, dear Lord, thy light, my star.
O let it lead me, lead me to thy feet !
So bring one gentile home.

Kings to thy rising came.
So, King of kings, I come to thee,
Yielding free homage at thy life-throned feet.
Flame life ! my life inflame.

I too, as gold, to thee,
Naught keeping back, my best would bring ;
Succoring all sorrow in His name who said,
So do ye unto me.

And when all prayers go up,
Parthean and Mede and farthest Ind,
North land and south land, with them, O may mine
Rise from that incense cup.

Then let my whole of life,
Fragrant with prayer and deeds as myrrh,
Be my last offering, Saviour, at thy shrine.
[So come, sweet end of strife]

(Lines found under a crucifix on the head-board of an ancient bed.

At thy feet, O wounded Christ,
    I would lie
As the seed beneath the harrow.
Self negate, for love thou diest ;
    Let me die
So to self. O pierce the marrow
   Of my rest with love's sweet pleading,
   Love divine, for others bleeding,
    Love of love's rewards unheeding,
    'Till the sky
Break where Jesus' lambs are feeding.

AT WHITSUNTIDE.

Spirit of good in all the past,
  Men ever leading upward to the light,
    Spirit of aspiration for the worthiest part,
      Oh, rest on me thy benison,—
In all thy being manifold, beyond or in our ken,—
  On every act and word and thought,
    On every consequent, and on us all,
      Now and forevermore. Amen.

Upward to the azure zenith
  Lark-like rose the glorious tone;
Fell in waves far down the vale,
  Where listening pines made answering moan.

Oh! 'twas wondrous! Hark, I cried,
  Nought so beauteous can endure;
Lo! upborne on eagles' pinions
  It soared on, glorious, strong and pure.

While I stood in listening wonder
  I recalled forgotten years,
Tones long hushed—than these more tender?
  Straight the tone changed—whence these tears?

Doubting still, though moved, I said,
  " In sordid souls, heroic fires
Voices have had power to wake."
  The song sang. " Shuman's Grenadiers."

I am vanquished! It hath done;
  Let none deny but envious churls,
All that voice can do, vain words!
  I heard with trembling flesh, " King Charles."

Through the window, through the garden,
  Out upon the terrace, came
Floating wild the wondrous voice,
  Ever changing, still the same.

Benedictus, oh! well named!
  Heaven blessed thou! its choice
Out of myriads, to possess
  The garden's sweetest flower—thy voice.

Alma Mater, mea Mater!
  When I come back to thy rest,
When the great blue dome rounds o'er me
  And the sun is in the west.

When o'er all the broad green campus
  Tender broods a trembling light,
And the faint, pale moon above me
  Waits the coming of the night;

When the dear trees stand back, fearing
Skies to hide, God made so fair,
And I drink in the great breath
Which I find, ah! only there.

When I, pausing, lest I fright
From my feet the tiny birds,
Look down o'er the pastures, fair
With homeward wending, silent herds ;

Look down o'er the foliage hiding
The broad breast of the ancient river,
Where the lovers' boats are gliding
Ever, for love lives forever.

When the distant little city's
Drowsy hum has died away,
And sunlit fires on slender spires
Mark the closing of the day.

When between the purple mountains
In the gorge, the fiery orb
Slowly sinks, and dying, sends
A flash of glory over all.

When he hovers on the brink,
Half is seen, is wholly lost,
When up from his amber-bed
The lights rush forth an arrowy host.

When the clouds are heaped up rubies,
Isles of fire in sapphire seas ;
When the glory tempts belief
* " Raphael hath found the keys."

Alma Mater, mea Mater,
In thy bounty, I find lack,
If returning to thee, never,
Sounds that voice my welcome back.

Mother, when my life is ended,
Let my head rest on thy breast ;
Let thy green sward be my cover,
When the sun is in the west.

---

* Raphael, the guardian angel of humanity, forever seeks the lost keys of the
gates of Paradise.

On the longest day of summer
Let his latest sunset ray
On me fall, where I lie waiting
For the never-ending day.

When my god his rest is seeking
Let them lay me, too, to rest;
Heap the red earth warm around me,
Range the sods above my breast.

Then, when the last word is spoken,
Let the weeping mourners stay,
If there be such, while that sweet voice
Chanteth for me a last lay.

Song of joy, or song of anguish,
Song of care, or song of rest,
Be the song she sings above me
Whate'er pleaseth her the best.

When 'tis ended, let who loves me
Each one flower lay on the sod:
Then to silence let all leave me—
Leave my soul alone with God.

Choirs of angels, choirs of angels
Rank on rank ascending high,
Bending o'er like corn in autumn
Bear me shouting through the sky!

Mater! Mater! hand outstretched—
Form invisible to me—
Leading where the great veil hideth
' What no human eye can see!

Faintly, faintly, a wild earth-cry
With the angelic choirs is blending,
Benedictus, benedictus
Jiületta's voice ascending.

TERRIBLE AS AN ARMY WITH BANNERS.

Cant vi : 4.

" Oh, they have a terrible beauty, those faces from over the sea."

(Mrs. Browning)

Over the crest of the hill gleamed the flash of their
    lances,

And in front of them, borne like a banner, the sound of
    the army advancing,

And the tramp of their horse and a sound as the
    breathing of many,

Came hushed on the fresh breath of morning in the
    stillness of summer.

And presently seen on the crest was the forefront ad-
    vancing in order,

In the terrible beauty and order of lines and battalions
    and columns ;

Not a mob without form and unmarshalled, but a pa-
    geant majestic and rhythmic.

Which swept down the slope, coming towards us slow,
    like a river of lava

Sent forth from some mighty volcano, resistless and
    solemn in beauty.

Now we distinguish the cannon and the men on the
    caisons behind them,

Riding roughly, and some of them laughing, some si-
    lent, and some riding friendly,

With their arms locked around one another ;

Or the cavalry riding in order, and many abreast in
    the breadth of the road ;

And the flash of their arms and their helmets ; and the
    flags of the guides and the pennants ;

And the stream of the infantry endless, their officers
    riding in silence ;

And the colors of regiments war-worn ; and the scarlet
    and gold of the bands ;
And the challenging blare of their trumpets, that woke
    all the echoes or died on the mountains,
While low throbbings musical filled all the air from the
    forests responding.

And the sun that had ridden for hours half veiled in
    the mists of the morning,
Broke forth in the fullness of glory, broke full on the
    army advancing,
And glorified all in his splendor, as the painters of old
    used to picture,
Arrayed in ineffable splendor, the innumerable hosts
    of the Blessed.
And while I stood watching that vision, harmonious and
    rhythmic in beauty,
The sound of the trumpets died on the mountains, the
    sound of the trumpets died in the forests,
And the bands sounded forth a great choral, such as
    sounds in St. Peter's at Easter,
And sobs rose in my throat and broke from me in a
    mute cry of pain.   On a sudden
My limbs seemed to fail to support me, and I clung
    where I stood, and the army went by me.
While I clung to the rail and the army went by me,
    my soul rose to God in thanksgiving !
Oh ! the pain of that sweetness, that splendor, that day,
    that ineffable moment.

Such was the power of rhythm,
Of mystic harmonious numbers,
And such was the terrible beauty
Of an army with banners!

―――――

[But last night I saw thee in a dream,Oh ! thou dear one,
Fairest of all on this earth, Oh, my lost one,
Passed now the stars beyond,
And lo ! thou wert more beautiful.]

AS I SAILED, AS I SAILED.

As I sailed, as I sailed
    The boundless main,
      Sailing lonely,
Just before the evening star
        Rose afar,
While yet the day was nearly done,
And red the waves were in the sun.
    And the air was balmy,
          Lo ! afar
     A full sailed ship,
Looming through the purple air.

Then I heard the beating, beating,
Of my great ship's heart,
And all her sails filled out responsive.
    And the white sails in the sun,
    Like to sails of gold they shone,
    And the ships were nearing, nearing,
      Nearing through the sunny air,
Fragrant all the zephyrs blowing,
Fragrance each to each bestowing,
      As from far
       We full sailed ships
Were nearing, through the purple air.
Now they towered, O they towered,
    Her stately mast trees,
      As gleaming spires,
And all her spars and tangled cordage
Were singled out against the sky
    As she came so nigh, so nigh.

And the narrowing seas between,
  Redder in the sunset shone.
And then a signal flag was seen,
    Then came a cry,
    Faint and far off
   Though we seemed so nigh,
And through the trumpet we called back
Salut to the ship saluting.

When my heart was beating, beating.
And my limbs were trembling, longing,
Fear and heaven in the meeting,
Wonder, love and longing thronging
Upward, struggling with my breathing,
Fancy's possible me wreathing
With its formless hopes and tremblings,
Was the gold light in the skies
But the glamour in mine eyes,
And the sudden flung-out signal
But the red flag in my cheek,
And love's ringing in mine ears
    The only trumpet?

Nearer in the golden even,
But we two 'twixt sea and heaven!
  O, how tender is the light!
  Day is dying into night,
  Day is yielding to the night.
Nothing now past joy or sorrow,
Nothing yestern or to-morrow,
  All is in abeyance ;
      Even thought
Stops a moment, for this moment
So with possible is fraught,
      Even thought
  Stops a moment.

O, the awe commencing session !
O, the longing for confession !
Tender hope of some concession,
Yet distrust of all profession !
O, the thrill before possession !
O, the sweetness of self cession !
O, come down, dear purple vapors,
Close around us, close around us ;
   So surround us
That the sky may never know ;
Shut out from us sea and sky.
 In thy misty perfumed light
 Hide us, till the coming night
  From all sight,
 Wrap us in his gracious veil ;
'Till his veil indulgent covers
  All the sea,
  As gracious be ;
Hide, O hide, my royal lovers.

II.

When the midnight stars were shining,
Side by side the ships reclining,
Lay at rest upon the ocean,
Rocked by waves in unison;
Nothing hoping, nothing fearing,
Nothing caring, nothing sharing.
Past the hopes and fears that thronging,
Thrill, the sweet unknown adorning :
Past the doubt, and past the longing.
Each was known and knew the other,
Each had found and lost a lover,
Each had memory sweet forever.

III.

After longest night the morning,
After sweetest dark, adorning
Comes the rosy light of morning,
All the eastern sky adorning.
From my prow the parting spray
Sparkles in returning day,
    Neither scorning,
    Nor yet mourning ;
All the past is far away,
All our thought is on our way,
On the journey of to-day.
Bright the deck beneath my feet,
And the morning is so sweet
    With every breath,
I ask if sorrow pain or death
Can ever come to me.
Above the horizon hangs afar
    The morning star,
   Paling in the growing light.
So, as splendors past take wing,
   The coming splendors come,
     I sing
    And know no care ;
    All life is fair,
    The past is dear,
    The present here,
I greet the future without fear,
    And onward sail ;
Far as the eye can reach,
    On every side
    A tossing plane,
Trackless and grey the billows lie,
Only my bark 'twixt sea and sky.

IV.

Yet, when the sunset comes again,
Sailing upon the jasper plane,
A sudden glamour in mine eyes
Makes tender hued the sea and skies.
Soft airs breathe perfumes, and again
I am not lonely on the main ;
Bound outspread from some far-off shore,
Stately the stranger comes once more,
  With tender thrill
   In memory still
Her rounded sails are seen,
   And still,
  But softer hued,
The waves run red between.

V.

Long years have passed; from shore to shore
My bark has tossed or voyaged sure,
Of perils past, of splendors seen,
Long is the record, and of praise and blame;
  On what has been
   I dare not cast
   The doubt of shame;
Sacred is every blessing of the past,
  Dear all the joy ;
So is the longing passion of that hour
 A thing for reverence.
That once found thrill was heaven to me,
 And reverently
Sometimes I think if heaven there be,
  We two shall meet,
  As then shall greet,
And sail together on the jasper sea.
Ah ! heaven were not to voyage for aye
Only my bark twixt sea and sky.

WEIGHING.

[Egisens, old, loq.]

When longings humour'd, thwarted,
Have robbed me of my beauty,
And feasts long since all ended
Have left but trace of blame.
        Moody, I weigh
The past against the present—
The wheat, once mine, devoured,
The husks that still remain.

        Yet, still I ask,
The dear lost past reviewing,
        Sacred in this,
That mine it was so sweet,
        What were my gain
If, with sad self denying,
        I had refused,
Enhungerèd to eat ;
        I had refused,
When I did thirst, to drink ?

        Or, what my gain,
Man's law for God's misplacing,
        Though I were filled,
Had I essayed the quelling,
        Nature's sweet thirst
With draughts I did not long for,
        Heaven given hunger
With that which was not bread ?

What were my gain.
E'en though I had been saving
As I have been spendthrift,
        Standing here to day?
        What were my gain,
Though barns were plenty,
        I having lost
The power to enjoy?

Or now, wherefore better
Were it, when my tear drops.
        Let I them fall.
Must fall o'er youth departed,
        That they should fall
As well o'er chances wasted ;
The past, the past—the future,
        Chances to come no more?
        What past soe'er, they fall
Alike o'er youth departed,
        O'er manhood's love days gone.

        Is it not better
To have burned than wasted ?
        Is it not better
Love spent to be than miss love ?
        Is it not better
To lose than ne'er to have ?

        Love's fragrant oil,
Life's dear lamp enriching,
        Is it not better
To have used than wasted ?
        Or is it better
To save to dry away ?

Loving and losing,
Still is it to be richer
Than love ne'er possessing.
Still to suffer loss ;
He who ne'er possesses
Suffers double loss.

Standing upon
The loveless land's drear threshold,
What were my gain,
To hear a voice repeating :
Lo ! the summer past,
And lo ! the harvest ended,
And you, you have not reapéd,
You have not even gleaned.
Not even gleaned,
Whom gods had made to gather !
Not even gleaned,
Whom gods had made to reap !

Save them O tender shepherds,
The lambs of life sweet guiding,
Save them at life's sad ending,
From such a dreary fate.
Me too, ye gods, still save ye
If not, alas, too late.

When these winter nights are o'er,
  I shall be
 Far away, where, far away,
When the winds breathe off the shore,
  Far out to sea
 They bear the fragrance of wild bay
And citron groves and palm fring'd woods,
 Where swing sweet ropes of emerald
  From tree to tree.
  That star set be
With countless perfum'd chalices
  Of golden jessamine.

· When here along this rugged coast
The storms beat wild and waves are tost
  High into air,
  Old ocean there
Will gather all his forces slow
In solemn swells that heave and flow
  Majestic, rhythmic, far between
And roll in grandly from far out to sea
Unerring to their destiny,
  Impelled by some vast thought unseen
Their caves of coral to forsake
And, when these winter nights are o'er,
  There, far away,
  On some sweet day,
To heave and swell and comb and break
In thunder musical along the strand
And die to silence in that perfum'd land.

 Ah ! when these winter nights are o'er,
Not e'en the self-same stars will hang
  Above us, thee and me.
 For me the southern cross will spangle heaven.
On thee, as now, this pole star coldly gleam.
 And e'en this moon, whose lance-like rays,
Reflected back from countless crystals of this endless snow.
 Makes path of silver to the far off sea,
 To thee as now a silver disk will seem,
 A shield of argent on an azure field,
  A blazon of some radiant race
  Painted on heaven's changing face.
 For me 'twill hang a glittering ball,

Sphcrèd, effulgent, dropping out of heaven,
Orbèd complete, suspended there in space,
   Hung far below the vaulted sky.

All will be different there, O love,
      Around, above,—within?
While here the hurrying crowds with thee,
The interests, cares, effacing me,
I there shall wander on, ah! dear,
Thy tender image ever near :
Careless of all but that from thee
I still must wander silently,
Far from thy thoughts, O love, as thee :
Always alone, apart from men,
Or still alone, though holding then
Converse, in accents strange to me,
With strangers grave that dreamily,
Aimless, still pass life's fragrant hours
Drifting among those pèrfum'd bowers.

And wilt thou then be mine, I dear as now,
      When these winter nights are o'er?
I cannot know, dear love, I cannot know,
But this I know that I am present now,
      I thine, thou mine, this hour our own.
      O, lose it not.   Love's hour is come,
The cup of love is full, love's rose full blown,
O, lay thy lips, twin roses, upon mine.
[All fires burn fiercer in this frosty air—
Thy kiss is warmer for the cold without.]
So ; clasp me closer in thy tender arms,
Thy breast to mine, till I am lost in thee.
Make we this moment safe and past all harms,
Past chance of loss, a loving memory,
      Ah, when these winter nights are o'er,
      A pèrfum'd memory.

The moments fly with wingèd feet,
The driver speeds his horses fleet ;
Unseen, hears he our pulses beat?
No, we are safe, alone, unseen,
Close curtain'd, warm.   So, nought between
Thy touch and mine, my fair, my fair,
O, hold me, hold me darling, there.
[Oh! if to feel our hearts thus beat
Be sin, why was it made so sweet ?]

REST.

Day after day I wandered forth ;
I wandered South and wandered North,
  I wandered East and wandered West,
  But no where found a place of rest.
    My worn heart wandered up and down,
    And found no place to lay it down ;
No place of blissful peaceful rest,
As on some fond and tender breast,
    To lay it down and rest,
       And rest.

Since North and South and East and West
I turned, and found no place of rest,
    In my despair to death I cried ;
    O Death ! since unto me denied
      Is rest, come thou ! thou bringst to me
      Oblivion, not eternity.
I cried, and from amid the blest,
One coming, clothed in glittering vest
    Spoke, pointing upward, Rest,
       Lo ! Rest.

Now day by day I go me forth,
And wandering South, and wandering north,
  And wandering East and wandering West,
  Have ever with me place of rest.
    What I had sought around, above
    Now have I found a home of love.
Careless of care, serenely blest,
Upon my Saviour's tender breast,
    Trustful I lie and rest,
       And rest.

DESPONDENCY.

"Shed no tear, shed no tear,
The flowers will bloom another year."
So the poet sang, and meant
Cheerful words with hope intent.
Yet cheerful words they're not to me,
For I ask where shall I be
When the spring will come again?
The flowers will bloom ; will I remain ?
If to-morrow or to-day,
I should die and pass away,—
Earth to earth, upon a clod
Heap the mould and lay the sod,
Then turn away and let him rot,
His aims, his hopes, himself forgot.

THE CHRISTIAN CHURCH.

The pure child rolls the snow ball in the fair snow.

It gathers and grows.   Others assist.

Bye and bye it is so cumberous and heavy that it

gathers, not only the pure snow, but much soil.

It is no longer a snow ball, though it passes for such;

Nor could the pure child any longer push it or recognize it.

Its weight would crush him if he fell under it.

(From Alessandro da Vainora.)

TO BENEFICENCE.

Come thou.   The tears are fallen, the complaining's done,
    The burial of Love is rung,
    The victory of Time is won,
And Love has fallen, and Love's requiem's sung,
    And time goes on ;
   And life has yet a space for me unfilled.

Unfilled for me who loved so well, so well !
[So well or ill, I ask not ; that is past.
Time brought the love, then took the love away,
Taking all love in taking power to love,
To love and win love ever back again.]

Fade far away, barge of the stately sails ;
Fade far away islands of perfumed rest.
Rest or unrest ye can not come again.
Fade far away.   Can ne'er return ?   Then fade.
[Bidden, or not, love's empire fades away.|

Come blessings to the world, blessings for each, for all !
All good life gave me I for all would seek ;
All pain life brought me, that from others shield,
    While life goes on,
   While life has yet a space for me unfilled.

FIRST OF THE TRAIN.

OF DUTY.

[From Alessandro da Vamora.]

First of the train,—best gift of all, that most,—
Most would I break all barriers down
Fold it from others, did I do His word
Bids me to do as I would be done by.
I may not hide the lesson of my life.

Love is life's best, beside which all is dross ;
And love is holiest in holiness,
Best when most true to nature, each to each,
And howe'er differing from prejudg'd dream,
How differing from all men's spoken thought.
That love is best which blesses most,
Most satisfies, and stills the soul with perfectness.

SONNET.

When in my happy home, which one alone,
  As all these years, can make complete with joy,
    I sup on fish, come thoughts I haste to drive
    Out from my mind, if that I can. I thrive
      On food, in home, both bought by suffering,—
        Nor mine. God of the fish and vestal, I
        Dare not thee question. No, I ask not why
    Nature and art are built on suffering,—
    My body, home where times I joyous sing
      All things forgetting but this joy : I live,
        And one I love o'er others lives with me.
        Yet did man's art, thy will, find ways to give
      Means, without pain or loss to aught, to live,
Fled were sad thoughts and I could only sing.

VESTALITY.

(From Alessandro da Vamora.)

VITTIMA :

    I did not say that Vestality was not often preferable to Mar-
       riage ; but I say that where Vestality is a fundamentum to
       Marriage.

    If I must be Vestal that you may be Married,
    I go to convents, thebetan or other,
    Lest the vale be o'er-peopled, the family fund
    Grow too small for pride, comfort,—whate'er value in Marriage,
    If I be the loser that you be the gainer,
    I must go childless that you know your children,
    Society's gain built on personal losses,
    To some all the gains, and to some all the losses,—
Well, 'tis well for the gainers,—but hard for the victims.

THE DREAMERS.

The Arch-communist :

I did not dream of a country where there was no sabbath ;
but I dreamed of a country where the sabbath was made for man,
and not man for the sabbath.

A Jesu-worshipper :

I did not dream of a country where there were no Institutions ;
but I dreamed of a country where institutions were valued for
what they were worth. I dreamed of a country where means
were not mistaken for ends.

A Radical :

I did not dream of a country where there was no marriage ;
but I dreamed of a country where marriage was honored and valued for the certainty it gave as to the fatherhood of children and the provision thus secured for their maintenance.

An advanced thinker :

I did not dream of a country where there were no vestals ;
but I dreamed of a country where vestality was not considered in
itself either a merit or a demerit.

An old statesman :

I did not dream of a country where there were no morals ;
but I dreamed of a country where morals were looked upon and
valued as means, not ends.

A Humanitarian :

I did not dream of a country where there was no hope of heaven ;
but I dreamed of a country where all behaved as well as if they
were in heaven.

A Conservative :

I did not dream of a country where there were no changes ;
but I dreamed of a country where the changes were improvements.
Nor did I dream of a country where there were no improvements ;
but I dreamed of a country where mere changes were not mistaken for improvements.

A tiresome person :

I did not dream of a country where there was no luxury ;
but I dreamed of a country where luxury consisted in the absence
of disagreeable things, and where " glory " (display and the
like) was considered vulgar, and waste stupid, and vulgar
and stupid things disagreeable.

A Gentleman of the old school :

I did not dream of a country where there was no press ;
but I dreamed of a country where newspapers, books, etc., followed much the same rules of good breeding as individuals,
and were no more intrusive, spying, personal, abusive, tattling,
detractive, indulgers in questions or comparisons than the
best bred individuals.

A traveller:

I did not dream of a country where there were no railroads;
 but I dreamed of a country where railroads were without noise,
  jar, dust, danger, incivility, door slamming, bad air, long walk
  at stations, no prompt delivery of luggage, or close and conven-
  ient correspondence with other vehicles; I even dreamed
  that each car in the train, like each camel in a caravan,
  might carry such burden as its individual master chose, and
  at such profit to him as he was individually satisfied with.

One who had been mistaken for a thief:

I did not dream of a country where there was no police;
 but I dreamed of a country where the police prevented crime without abusing criminals, or others.
   I dreamed of uses, not abuses.

An old Superior Court Justice:

I did not dream of a country where there were no courts;
 but I dreamed of a country where courts of conciliation preceded
  and, by keeping the combatants apart, generally evitated,
  often by the services of one man or woman only, at mere nom-
  inal cost, all appeal to other courts or arbitrators.
   I dreamed, not of what is arbitrary, but of what is reason-
   able, and so is convincing, and so is conciliatory.
   I dreamed of the ART of Peace, not War.

A Thoughtful Jailor:

I did not dream of a country where there were no convicts;
 but I dreamed of a country where convicts might earn all they
  could, and at any employment they chose (compatible with
  keeping them sequestered from harming the community by
  crime), and might make such honest use of their earnings as
  they thought proper.
   I dreamed, not of vengeance; but of protecting the community.
  And I even dreamed of placing convicts in conditions most
  adapted to help them to become good and useful citizens.

A middle-aged woman:

I did not dream of a country where women were equal to men;
 but I dreamed of a country where women might do, without in-
  curring opprobrium, any work which they could do fairly
  well.

A Philosopher:

I did not dream of a country where there was no love of man for
  man nor woman for woman;
 but I dreamed of a country where such a love was esteemed or dis-
  esteemed in proportion as it embodied or lacked noble and
  ennobling qualities.

An aged physician :

I did not dream of a civilization where there was no crime or secret vice ;

but I dreamed of a civilization that was not, as is ours, the creator of the one and founded on the other.

An old teacher :

I did not dream of a country where all agreed exactly as to what was or was not decorous ;

but I dreamed of a country where all endeavored to avoid any wound to the sense of decorum of others, and where this courtesy was not mistaken for any other virtue or right.

A Child of Light :

I did not dream of a country where there was no criticism of writings, music, art, methods, manners, or morals ;

but I dreamed of a country where partisanship, and partisan utterances, and mere gossip about producers, was not offered, still less applauded, accepted, and mistaken for, criticism of products.

A Statistician :

I did not dream of a country where they put artificial and cruel checks on population :

but I dreamed of many countries soon deeming it unwise to officially insist on the continuance of any artificial stimulus to population, now become unnecessary, often undesirable, and sometimes cruel.

A Scoffer :

I did not dream of a country where there were no priests of old religions :

but I dreamed of a country, many countries, where such priests wheeled 'round and squared with new ideas,—the dull or simple reluctantly, the clever or self-seeking ardently,—just as their like have ever done and ever will do.

A Paragraphist :

I did not dream of a country where there was no amusement over other folk's misfortune and comical sufferings ;

but I dreamed of a country where such amusement did not [as did the Greeks' amusement at the comicality of Thersites' dirty tear-stained face, when Agamemnon slapped him for protesting against the wrong done to Achilles, in forcibly taking his Briseïs away from him] prevent folk uniting against, and preventing, unfairness and cruelty.

All the Accused, together, thoughtfully :

I did not dream as one who sleeps ;

but I dreamed as one whose eyes are open and who reads the signs of the times.

A Philanthropist :

I did not dream of a country where no one did evil who found it to
his interest to do evil ;

but I dreamed of a country where the removal of men's interest to
do evil was practiced as the easiest way to do away with evil.

THE VICTIMS.

[A PROSAIC STATEMENT.]

Whatever the plan, whatever the system,
Whate'er the machine, or whate'er the invention,
Whatever its merits, its gain in the gross,
It will have its defects—found out sooner or later.

Men gain by it? Well. But what of the victims,
On whom fall less heavy the gains than the losses?
Pass by them? They're silent. Pass by them unconscious.
Pass by? They are weeping. Pass by unregarding?

Vain thought! On perception will follow comparing;
Then perception of values; then blame or approval.
Then quick comes the question: This blame, on whom resting?
On what person or persons, what system or systems?

Vain the hope of more sleep, of a little more slumber!
To the ant, or man's wit, flies the wise, creeps the sluggard.
No resting, no peace for conservative folk,
'Till a new system's found, or the old system's mended.

Then a respite may last—'till the new system's morrow
Brings the groans of its victims, the new cry of sorrow.
But the wheel must go 'round while a victim is weeping;
No rest for the wakeful, short sleep for the sleeping,

Be it so. Let but death be the sleep knows no waking
To pity, to help. Not the victims forsaking
But succoring alone can bring peace to man's breast,
The last victim's last sob bring humanity's Rest.

[From Alessandro da Vernora.]

THE BEST WAY, OR MY WAY.

[A PART OF A LETTER.]

The good in things does not justify retaining them ;
nothing short of perfection will justify retaining them.
We can only retain them with satisfaction until we can
get something better ; we must regard them, most things,
as temporary, as stop-gaps, until better things, or ways
with which to do their work, or a better work, are found.

We need not lay down, as if forever or at all, the old way ;
Only, we must not let retaining the old way, hinder
the adoption of a new. There are losses as well as gains
incident to probably every change ; but we must count,
or try to count, or at any rate be willing to count,
the gains as well as the losses, the losses as well
as the gains. Doubtless some will have an eye
only for one and not the other ; but this will not justify
him whose eye is wholly or mostly on the losses
in hindering him whose eye is wholly on the gains.

He must but hinder harm to others and himself,
Not solely hinder others' chance of blessing lest
Himself be harm'd. He must not even careless risk
Great harm to others, to give self a little good.
No way to work together found, let each him seek
How best himself, in his own way, to work. This does
The doctrine, fact, of motions Independence teach
In its philosophy ; which, too, ships' tackings teach
In practice. Do not interfere in haste, prevent,
Because the ship seems sailing in direction quite
Away from the desired haven. Heed the wise.*

Each method has its value, new or old ;
This Indian shawl, this hand-made lace, possess
Beauty and charm machine-made fabrics lack.
This shawl not Indian ? This not hand-made lace ?
Alas for me, my judgment, pride, or purse.
Yet happy they who can possess the charm
Of shawls and lace like these—their greatest harm
They seem'd those made by hand or Indian loom,
(For whose real charm the world, too, findeth room,) –
Happy, these now in reach. In moral things,
Methods, machines, invention too hath wings.
Faiths change, then manners, men the best hold fast
Only while each man's-best-conceiv'd shall last.
Old methods left behind, all changes, tell
The tacking of the ship, man's history. Farewell ?

* I think I have noticed that most affirmative propositions contain truth, most
negative ones the contrary.—EMERSON.

No, not farewell while spiritual bliss
Or, higher still, the spirit's worthiness
You hold to justify, at every cost,
All suffering. The world's well lost
Only when something better's gained.
Nor then well lost if that might gained be
Without the sacrifice. Oh! wearily
They cudgel'd children's brains, who taught by rote.

To feel, to suffer, seek assuagement, find,
Find twice, compare, prove all things, keep the best's,
The law and history of living things.
All count the cost, and each one seeks to know
How to live happiest. Some men, here below,
Heav'n blest to gain, hang them to trees by hooks
Rived through their flesh; in sacrifice,
In loss, with no gain visible on earth,
In loss of comfort, cheer, amusement, rest,
Would purchase Heaven; so, they seek the best.
Others, of discipline, not sacrifice,
Speak, seeking weary ways to justify;
So, count the cost. They: " Daily exercise
That wearies, irks, has yet its worth in health
It brings to body, discipline of soul."
Yes, but when ways are found to get like gains,
Such health of body, discipline of soul,
By ways less tiresome, long, or full of pain,
If I still choose the longer painful route,
And close all other routes to other men,
'Tis imperception, not perception, friend,
Ignoble mind-work if from lack of thought,
Ignoble feeling if from pain through wound
Received to self esteem that other men
Should find a better road than I in plan
Resolv'd to walk in for the goal I'd gain.
Yet, t'were not folly so yourself to walk,
An't please ye. Walk so. But, kind friend, be kind.

Or blind friend is it? Wish ye to be blind?
So, now at last, farewell? A little prayer?
A little self-effacement? Strength to say:
Not my way, but the best way, Lord, alway?

Yet, all the while I know, full well I know,
Him wise who counts the gains where he must go;
Uses old ways, their worth well known; is slow
To change in act; yet, while he walketh so,
Shuts eyes nor ears to betterment. 'Twere right
To shut out every other way from sight?
His sight or others'? If he walk in night,
Should he prevent, permit, a way of Light?

HYMN.

[Air: My Country (God save the King).]

Humanity, of thee,
Crownèd with Liberty,
  Of thee I sing.

    Though long the hours may wait,
    'Twill come, or soon or late,
    The hour ordain'd of fate
      With thee our king.

Then be thy ways as light:
Taught of the antique night,
  Seek truth for all,

    Justice for everyone,
    For all beneath the sun :
    So let thy will be done,
      All good for all.

THE LOST LORD.

Thoughtless and gay was I, long years ago,
    Lighthearted too!
With undimmed eyes I looked upon the world,
    And sky of blue.
In songs of praise, my waking soul burst forth,
    At early light ;
With grateful heart I closed confiding eyes,
    On darkening night ;
As wearied child from play, with folded hands
    On mother's breast ;
Or home returning bird on tired wings
    To peaceful nest.
I sought with sages deeply hidden truths,
    In wisdom stored;
Enchanted, dazzled with the treasure trove,
    I lost my Lord !

Now, days returning, like ships come to port,
    My soul is mute ;
And darkness settles with far twinkling stars,
    In pain acute ;
I care not for the beauteous robe or crown,
    The perfume sweet,
The thrill of music or the scattered flowers,
    About his feet ;

I do not care to know his parentage,
     Or whence he came,
Or seek long lonely hours what meaning hid,
     In mystic name.
My eyes, with light bewildered, of each day,
     Inquire in vain.
The unresponsive night comes on, and all
     Is dark again.
I trace his footprints where the wretched are,
     Where sorrow is,
I know he has been there, because the light
     Is surely his ;
Has been, alas! but is not, and my heart,
     Perplexed with doubt,
Through cold and darkness groping seeks in vain,
     My Lord without,
Thus haply, if I follow where I know
     That he has been,
On some sweet morrow, I may wake and find,
     My Lord within.

"NATIVE MOMENTS."

The truth eternal standing there
  Looked back, looked deep into my eyes
    And would be known.

    Acknowledge me,
    Who made thee, thou thyself, or God!
Nay, thou hast heard my voice all, all along.
Whence came the love that has consumed thy heart,
Whence came the longing all the lagging years,
The sense of unfulfilled, of best untried :
    Who made thee, thou thyself, or God!
Who gave the bliss, who crowned the cup,
Who made the draught so sweet, so sweet,
Which is the sweetest mercy of thy life?
    Who made thee, thou thyself, or God!

The truth eternal standing there
  Looked back, looked deep into my eyes.
    And would be known.

AS YEARS ROLL ON.

PROCESSIONAL.

[Decani and Cantoris, approaching from different aisles :]

Breaking 'gainst rocks of a rock bound land,
Rippling over a shingly strand,
Gliding up a silvery sand
So the years roll on.

Can. Stain'd oft with blood the smuggler's cave ;
Sorrow and sin, as wild storms, rave ;
They won and they lost, those smugglers brave ;
So did the years roll on.

Dec. Wedded for love, or lone of heart,
Each life must patient bear its part,
Bringeth it joy or only smart,
So do the years roll on.

Can. Robber chieftain, or baron bold
King, or capitalist, 'twas told :
Theirs of right all their hands can hold ;
So the years must roll on.

Dec. Home convenience and interest
Fix all fates ; this way is the best.
Some must yield to give life its zest ;
So the years will roll on.

[Together in the nave :]

Can. No new truth can ever be foal'd.
Dec. All is known and everything told.
Dec. and Can. Changeless thus have centuries roll'd.
So the years roll on.

[After a time the choirs are seen, like the returning shuttle, approaching from the opposite direction.]

Dec. and Can.   Far and faint their memories now.
Can.   Smuggling's gone.
Dec.   And shame on the brow.
Dec. and Can.   Strange survivals they were I trow.
So the years roll on.

Passing together down the nave :

Breaking 'gainst rocks of a rock-bound land,
Rippling over a shingly strand,
Gliding up a silvery sand,
So waves and years roll on.

STANZA.

O time! O fate! O Providence of good!
Slow is thy foot, though succor thou shouldst bring,
If, bringing succor, still on victim's pain thy footsteps press.
Hasten! Heed not the scoff " They would the world new made ;
And in a day." Where'er the old gives pain it asks the new.
Wherein the new is better, hasten well its day.
Lighten the load, where load is. So. Alway.

WHERE THERE IS SUFFERING.

[From Alessandro da Vermora.]

Though men proclaim them, as of wont of old,
I cannot know—I cannot think I know—
Th' eternal purposes.   Mine eyes are dim?
Or seems the way shut in?   Alike, the far,
The ultimate, I cannot see—I cannot seem to see,
The while close by me sobs a sufferer.

Eternal purpose pardon me if, stooping low
Or straining upward, I essay the pain t'assuage,
The withe that binds to loosen, weights remove;
So, move athwart th' eternal purposes
I cannot see, or think I cannot see.

INFLEXIBLE FACTORS.

He toss'd the baby lightly in his arms,
   Forgetful of the chandelier above its head ;
Th' unyielding bronze, the baby's soft skull, met.
   Unharmed's the bronze, there. But the baby's dead.

A quivering mold of aspic crown'd a plat
   With silver skewers pierced, the table's pride.
As borne in past, a skewer Jack grasp'd, held firm ;
   Which rent the fabric. "Spoilt!" the butler sigh'd.

For streets symmetric, straight. lots uniform of size,
   Sufficient for all average needs the fathers had an eye ;
But not for needs, alas, as small as yours and mine.
   So now in stifling tenements we suffocate and die.

In what they seek t' effect, men often are well taught ;
   In what t' avoid, as oft, but children ne'er at school.
The yielding factors yield, some crush, whenever men
   Some factor introduce of changeless iron rule.

With things "intended well" ev'n hell is pav'd 'tis said,
   "Who'd do no evil, then, must naught do?" asks Alarm.—
Where all is flexible, most harms are quickly shunned ;
   One hard-fast-rule or factor—*then comes endless harm.*

THE UNSEEN PRESENCE OF THE ONE I LOVE.

O presence, unseen presence of the one I love !
Music unheard, but never absent from my breast !
O golden days, made golden by a dream,
A dream unspoken, half unformed, a dream
So pure, so sweet, so precious every hour,
Whispering the unseen presence of the one I love !.

A COMING CHANGE AND THE POETS OF THE FUTURE.

Swift come the rolling years.
Yet, soon to come,—so soon to come,—
A change far greater than the years have known
For long and long moves toward us.   Who could dream
When (from the orient?) first gun's powder came,
Man's self-defence given up to body politic,
Woman's defence assured (then ill perceived),—
Upon it close would follow swift,—so swift,
Four hundred years, a breath, in time,—her call,
Self issued, for self-help, then sole support?
Then, swifter, will to sole support
Her offspring, rather than be stayed,—if sted
By trammel in the staying, sted no more?
Then, swifter than outreaching eye can see,
Comes trammel past, freedom in one more way
Added to freedoms past slowly evolv'd
Or won by man as mass from separate men.

Old withes unbound, breaking of withes is past.
Old sins are no more sins with old laws dead.

Sin's strength, the law, now abrogate, new fields
Must minstrel, player, story-teller find.

No tale to tell when love alone will bind?
Stay! Love is fairest in love's utterest;
Love will touch hearts while hearts can beat with love,
Life will go on more fair, more pure, more real,
Though, like " the Lord's anointed," as a dream
Will seem the-king-must-not-be-touched, (yet whom
To touch, yet leave untouched, were all the aim
Of romancist and singers ages past).
King now no more! touch'd, gone for aye,

The antique king of romance, love and duty,
Striving and striving in an endless strain !
While, king for aye while human hearts can love,
Love will remain, best gift of heaven to men.

Haste then, slight book, whisper your passing strain
While it has life,—it cannot live again ;
Tell of submission when the heart is wrung,
Tell of desertion when the heart hath sung,
Tell of love living as t'will live for aye
When what inspires towers toward the sky.
Tell of the wars, for soon war will be o'er,
Tell of the voyage toward the eternal shore,
Tell of the tears,—the tears that soon must cease,
Tell of the smiles,—the eternal smiles of peace.

STANZAS.

The grains of sand roll down, roll down
The grains of sand roll down toward the sea.
The grains of sand lodge curiously.
    (Ah, me! for me!
The grains of sand lodge curiously for me.)

The grains of sand pile up, pile up,
As if forgetful of the far off sea,
'Till starts the lodgement.   Furiously
The grains of sand then rush toward the sea.
    (Heedless of me!—
The grains of sand rush on toward the sea.)

I know not sweet ensample, elder brother, friend,
If thou art conscious now, yet still I fain would wend
   Sure steps that toward thee meeting, Saviour, tend.
Meeting with thy sweet likeness, or thy sweeter self?
I know not, ask not. E'en, without other prize or pelf,
   Still would I fain do well because 'tis well,
Shun pain for self, for all, fearing no other hell.
     Nor didst thou bid me self to seek,
     By thine ensample, Saviour meek ;
     Nor sacrifice, nor self, thine aim ;
     But blessing only. Heavenly flame,
  Howsoe'er lighted, burning in human breast,
  Burn not in vain in mine.
               Is there no rest?
No ending of the burning of love's flame?
    No work all done? No, not while life,
    'Twixt good and evil, as an endless strife,
    'Twixt joy and pain, 'twixt weariness and doubt,
    Swings like some pendulum.
             Lo, in the west
The sun is sinking and the day is gone.
Oh, when my sun is sinking, and my day is done,
  Let me not have to say : Those that forlorn
I found, I left as wretched as I found. That thorn
  Press not, oh fate, against my dying breast.
  While life lasts, work. In but death only, rest.

ASPIRATION.

Always will men aspire, all beings too,
Always reach upward for the highest known,
Or highest dream'd of, be it earthly good,
Or Heav'n, more fair than earth, beyond the skies.
To-day is heav'n regarded as a dream?
Men seek to make a second Heav'n of earth,--
As voyagers turn to deck their place of birth,
Make it an El Dorado, home of joy and rest
Find they, or ne'er, the El Dorado of their ancient quest.

As those led by a way that they knew not we evolv'd these poems,
As emerging in unsought chamber from some winding stair,
As wand'ring from int'rest to int'rest through glen thickly wooded,
By turns gath'ring leaflet or pebble, burr or flow'ret that beckon'd
us onward.
As one turns when the daylight is fading, finds the way he has come
by o'ershadow'd,
The spot where he stands unexpected, reluctant to part with his
gleanings,
Finds a way forth to carry them safely yet leave his hands free for
his journey,
So here are bound up these reminders. We keep, haply bury them
here,
Each recalling a moment of joyance or thought; now a smile, now
a tear,
Now a seeking of methods of blessing, now of shunning a danger
anear
Or afar, and or dreaded, unnoted. In joy learning joy of posses-
sion,
In loss learning sorrow of loss, aye the golden rule pleading for
others,
The pendulum swinging, so pass'd we, by ways that we knew not led
onward,
Made glad as we pass'd by the pleasures and int'rests that onward
way brought us.
Who led by a way that we knew not, or what force impell'd,
Blind Fate, or a loving Father, conscious, unconscious power?
Though we know not nor dare to question, though be ours rightly
praise or blame,
Dear the gift that each moment brought us, each meed of the passing
hour,
Each charm and each interest—which greater?—far away, scarce
recall'd now. The flame
Of the sunset glow warns us our journey together is ending. Each
henceforth
His sep'rate way home must be wending. So now when the daylight
is fading,

When the moment of parting approaches, ere leaving the past far
    behind us,
Exchange we as tablets these fragments, stain'd leaflets and bark
    films, recalling
Joy, int'rest, or effort, so garner'd may haply be gleanings of worth
    still
To those chance to heed them.   Farewell.   Part we here now and
    some for long voyages,
Outward bound t'ward the islets of silence, outward bound 'cross the
    seas to new fields,
And as mariners watching still ever from the prow what the horizon
    yields,
As mariners still ever hoping, sailing on as with sails unfurl'd,
Each morn will a new fairer morrow bring forth for a waiting world.

CONCLUDING NOTE.

In gathering together, or reviewing, the pieces which make up this brief volume, we find them, although written at different times, and not all by the same hands, yet having a certain likeness in the underlying thought which animates so many of them as seems to justify, nay, when once suggested, almost to compel, the title given to the collection.

In the NOTE, prefatory to the Poems, the uncertainty of duration of all things earthly, and so the rise, reign, and passing away, one after another, of results of various Factors, for a time held to as Inflexible,—and such as have been, each in turn, deemed highly important, or even necessary, to various human societies—is brought forward.

In the PRELUDE the different aspects which such Factors take in our minds under varying Circumstances is dwelt upon.

In the SUITES, in cases entirely separate in circumstances, scenes, and personæ, are seen effects of enactments which, whether held as human or divine, have been held as imposed on conscience as Inflexible Factors. Thus the AGRALAIDE is made up of fragments contributing toward a picture of a passion, beautiful and ennobling in itself, but sacrificed by its Subject to a call of conscience. The EGLANTINE consists of fragments contributing toward a picture of a passion, delicate and pure in itself, but sacrificed by its Object to the call of conscience. In the THREE WINDS is seen an attempted suppression of all earthly love or passion by its Subject at the call of conscience. In ACHRALAL a passion turned in upon itself is then seen unpremeditatedly fixing itself, unreturned, upon a passing Object and questioning of duty. As DIFFERING LINKS ENCHAINED shows the agitation and fluctuation of mind following on passion gratified, in reality or in intention, Contrary to conscience. IN A GARDEN is composed of fragments faintly picturing a lot Blessed of Earth and Heaven. The next suite touches on the Season of love ; the next on Temperament ; and the next on the differences in personal characteristics at Different Ages. In AFTER THE SUMMER IS ENDED a poetic parallel is suggested between similar Forces in Nature ; and effects from the same force, when acting on different natures, are contrasted.

Whatever relates to the sentiment or passion of Love lends itself, more than do other subjects, to poetic treatment, as is shown by its being the subject of by far the greater number of lyrical poems, as well as of plays and romances innumerable, throughout history. Poems on that subject are, in any volume of verses, likely to be those most numerous ; and this would doubtless have been the case here

therefore, even if all the poems had been by one instead of by several writers. Yet the subject of the Diptych entitled PRACTICALITY has occupied in both the head and heart of one of the writers, by many times over, all the attention probably given to other subjects. While again a multiplicity of subjects such as those named in THE DREAMERS, which have occupied much attention as affected by Factors seemingly Inflexible, not only did not, by their nature seem to lend themselves to lyrical treatment, but besides, seemed, when having a place in such a collection, best treated in such a way as to give the results of that attention stated in the most condensed and brief form.

Throughout the majority of the pieces it is the bearing or the results of Inflexible Factors of various kinds which most generally are dwelt on ; and then, further, the habit of mind is dwelt on which resents change, even for the better, in that which is established and customary. And the reason often of this habit of mind is hinted at ; and the value and importance of this resentment is compared to the pain of victims, under whatever System such pains have been, or are now, made necessary. And the willingness to study to amend any System, so as to secure its advantages, where that is still desirable, while eliminating its evils, its creation of victims, is so, by implication, put forward as a disposition of mind, not indeed unusual, but as not yet so usual as is that general sentiment of pity for suffering, and desire to avoid inflicting it, now so commonly evidenced among men.

We all wish that suffering may be avoided ; but we all tend to take refuge (from the wearying duty of seeking how it may be avoided) in thinking it unavoidable. If sufferings which we deplore are inevitable under existing enactments or conditions, it rests us, because it relieves us of responsibility, to think of those enactments or conditions as something fixed, and as unalterable as the laws of the Medes and Persians. Doubtless, in a comparatively early stage of Society the sense of security given by a general agreement that laws, once established, should never be changed, had its value, its great value. But those conditions of society are, as a general rule, with us at least, long past. In shipwreck the company often, we are told, agree to obey such a leader as they may choose, implicitly ; and there is doubtless a time for inflexibility of law, just as there is a time for a dictator. But when the time comes that the need of inflexibility of laws, or need of dictators, is past, the disadvantages they bring with them come to the front, and men modify laws and depose dictators. Such depositions may be made with violence, as in the French Revolution and as generally when resistance to change is stubborn and implacable ; or may be made almost unconsciously, as often in happier instances in the history of the human race. Once men, their own happiness secured, paid little attention to the sufferings and losses involved in securing it. Something of this still exists, in a striking form, in the East, as seen in its slave trade, and slave system, and the uses made of the slaves. But the feeling of

occidental nations toward oriental slavery shows how far such an indifference to the sufferings, uses, or maiming of human beings, is from the present thinking of the more civilized of mankind.

A study of the law or fact of the Independence of Motions, once intelligently made, and a sense of the parallel that exists between all *arrangements* whether material or moral—which is indeed at the base of our more modern systems of instruction, from the kindergarten upward—must lead, it seems to the writer, any student having also at all the inventive faculty, to a habit of mind which will lead him to think that any fault in any machine is something which most likely can be gotten over, and so is something which men, using their best powers, ought to seek to overcome,—and this whether the machine, the contrivance, the method, is one used for material or moral ends. So, to that high sense of duty which led the Medes and Persians to hold as unchangeable their laws, succeeds, in our day, that sense of duty so to perfect law that it presses hardly on none.

That law should press hardly on some was the antique view of right, finding expression in antique art, in their caryatidæ, their " Persians " bending in suffering and tears under heavy burdens. It is fine—from their point of view. It is the reign of law made visible. But, just as the Greeks at last made their caryatidæ beautiful, bearing their burdens lightly, and so marked a progress, for the time, in human thought, in man's consideration of his fellows, or—if we choose—man's view of what it is pleasing to himself to contemplate, so now we cannot contemplate suffering,—either presented in antique works, or in a mediæval campo-santo, or in a Last Judgment carved around a cathedral door,—with entire sympathy. We look upon all that as the art expression of its time.

And, if we cannot bring ourselves to express such sufferings now in art, neither can we, with comfort, contemplate in imagination any form of suffering, once we have thought of it as suffering. Nor can we think with comfort of any form of suffering as inevitable, once we have thought of it as evitable. Nor can we, having once thought of any form of evil or suffering as evitable, continue to live on contentedly without striving to hasten the day when it will be evitated.

Where the results of Inflexible Factors are only, or mainly, happy, it is indeed as if one lived delightfully, in his own house, mid gardens, in the city of his choice; but, where those results are otherwise, it is as if one pined and stifled in a faulty tenement-house in the city, not of his choice so much as of his enslavement. And as those living in delightful homes may yet pity, and even desire to rescue, those living in faulty and stifling tenements, so too it is natural that any form of suffering should, if once seen, and anywhere about them, touch the hearts of those, whether writers or readers, who live in joy.

If, as is suggested in one of the papers in the Appendix to this volume, the experience of mankind has been that of man both in a

collective and individual capacity gradually learning to let others alone in order to be himself let alone, [a selfish lesson—yet a lesson in self-restraint, a lesson in foregoing a pleasure, the pleasure almost the most grateful and tempting to active minds, that namely of meddling and interfering with others, and governing others, and so bringing about results which seem to one's self desirable, whether desirable for self or others,] if the experience of man has been to learn somewhat to govern his conduct, whether in an individual capacity, or when acting with others, by this lesson, yet still vast masses when acting collectively, and most individuals when thinking about a vast number of subjects have not arrived at a knowledge of this lesson, still less at its practice.

Nothing would seem simpler than that folk should not in a collective capacity impose ill-judged restrictions on their own individual convenience of action, rather than, like their ancestors, hasten to do so in the hope (often mistaken) of some selfish advantage, and then vainly strive to ease their own resultant sufferings, and to right themselves, by maltreating their own instruments (kings, ministers, classes,) in occasional revolutions. But to perceive this seems only given to the few; and the few, in the progress of mankind, are necessarily continually being swamped by the many. Probably to some always is given a cheerful common sense, so caution (in accepting and acting on theories, since theories are many while there can be but one Truth), hence inaction (in restraining others), self-restraint, *temperance*,—the result, aimed at, a Golden Age. Always, certainly, to others is given zealotry (often morose), action in restraining others, *self-worship*, intemperance,—and results achieved like the Nuremberg Dogberrys' torture chambers, and the Inquisition. Wise inaction is forgotten. Unwise action lives in its dreadful products.

We must expect therefore—however many the sermons, at various times and in various places, preached, like this one, on this subject —that for long and long the majority of mankind, as in the past, will, on the slightest provocation, and in proportion as they have opportunity, rush into Hindering and Imposing of Restrictions and such like Law or Rule making, of various kinds civil or social. Then, little by little, and sometimes, alas, very long afterward, we must expect one and another to perceive the evil effects which have, unforeseen, grown out of such restrictions and laws and interferences,—effects which in congestion and suffering of parts or even destruction of parts, have been suffered from often for long, for a generation, for centuries, for ages, without their connection with the laws or restrictions which have bred them being generally, or perhaps at all, perceived. Then, slowly,—after vast evil has been done, evil which can never be atoned for, never made up for to the victims, the generations, the individuals, that have lived and died suffering from those evil effects, the cause of all this suffering will be removed in the shape of some ill-considered and never necessary, or at best like female foot-binding in China, only temporarily useful, Inflexible Factor.

A THEORY

OF

THE ORIGIN OF

ORGANIC FORM

A paper read before members of the Faculty of Columbia College and others, New York, November 5, 1875.

———— •◦•— ————

Break an egg. The white and the yelk we are told each is a mass, in which no certain trace of the future chicken can be found. Whether this is so or not, yet by heat, a hen's or a furnace's, the full fledged chicken is brought forth. Why not some other form? The object of this paper is to answer that question.

In the autumn of 1868 I saw in London some of the beautiful Venetian glass made by Salviati at Murano, and while examining it, it occurred to me that it furnished an explanation of the likeness of child to parent. There seems to be a general notion, now-a-days, that force and matter are interchangeable, and that the different proportions of the inherent force in the atoms of carbon, oxygen and hydrogen, for example, make a combination of them, as albumen, for instance, organic, absorbative. We can conceive of clots of absorbative matter increasing in bulk till they fall apart from their own lack of adhesiveness, so propagate. Divers conditions develop in them divers organs or diversions in their organization—in ages developing more and more complicated beings, individuals in each generation inheriting the extremest complications of the preceding—like father like son. But why like father like son?

The why is evident to the Venetian glass student. Take a a molten stick of glass, one end white the other red. Double it upon itself. Draw out the new stick so formed, half red half white, to the finest thread. Examine it through a microscope.

The white and red are there as distinct as ever. Double it again and draw out the thread, or stick so formed, to however attenuated a hair. Two whites, two reds are visible, and so on ad infinitum. The *relative relations* of the atoms of matter to each other never change. New relations can be formed, but the old remain. Take a figure, in plan say a star; deposit on one point red glass, on another blue, on another yellow, on another white, on another green. Fill around the points with black glass. When molten and the whole is fused together it will make one stick of glass, which can be while ductile drawn out to the finest conceivable thread, but break it off anywhere and examine the end of the thread and the star will be there. When the thread is extended by a force acting equally on all parts of its section the relative position of the atoms is un-unchanged. Such is the experience with Venetian glass. Such is the experience with all ductiles. Such we can conceive to be the law of homogeneous matter. The same law would hold if the glass were colorless, but we could not see the fact. It would seem one homogeneous stick of glass. It would be, but the relative position of its atoms would remain like the parent star, though the fact would not be made visible. So it is with the egg or the germ within it. Its atoms all have the relative position of those of the parent from which it was secreted. Yet it may seem or be a homogeneous mass, and if colorless, the chicken in it, or rather the chicken that it is, will be as invisible as the star when its points are all of white glass.

Take a minute portion of the thread containing the colored star, and suppose the glass were absorbative, and absorbed from the atmosphere, or other matter with which it came in contact, matter like itself. If it absorbed equally all over, which with like conditions in its parts of itself, and like conditions in its surroundings it must do, then the almost invisible fine star in the minute fragment of thread would grow to be a large but similar star, and ultimately obtain the size of its parent. The same would be true of a bit of the thread of the colorless star. So the chicken in the egg grows into a big chicken. The chicken is invisible in it because transparent, colorless, like the invisible star present in the white glass, but its several parts are all there. If it grows at all it must grow to be like its parent.

Every part of my body is alive. The blood drawn from my arm is alive—organic. If I set it away where it will not dry up too fast, it will breed, or at least feed animalculæ, maggots, etc., and so live. I am a collection of lives, but I have an individuality, just as the United States has, though composed of separate States, and they of counties, they of townships, peoples, houses, lands, etc., etc. Any part of me, separated from me, goes on living. It may further separate, disintegrate into atoms and separate organisms, as it does if it rot. Or it may be absorbed into other lives as is the mother's milk. But only that which bears the impress of all of me can go on living like me. I can fuse the stick of glass containing the star, and draw from it a thread of the red, the blue, or the white, but only the thread drawn from every part of the star will contain the whole star. Only the secretion from the whole plant bears the impress of the whole plant. Only the secretion from the whole and fully developed plant, (bearing the impress of all of it, therefore), is the seed or germ. That is the definition of a seed or germ in fact. A definition, so far as I know, never before given.

The leaf is organic. If it falls it rots, and is usufructuous. It cannot develop into anything. It could only develop into a leaf, and it is a leaf already. A leaf cannot give forth new leaves. It stays a leaf till it dies. So of a bit of the bark, or any other bit larger or smaller, bearing only the impress of a part of the plant. But take a part bearing the impress of all the organs, it grows to display all the organs. Take the seed or a branch. It has all the organs of the plant hidden in it. It can grow ; and the branch or the seed, the smallest form of branch, containing all the organs in its folds, must grow into the likeness of its parent. It is like the minute bit of star-containing glass, which could only grow (if it grew) into the bigger similar star.

Distance, space, are only relative. Finite mind cannot follow into the infinite smallness of the parts of the star, in the thread so attenuated as to be invisible to which we can conceive the glass drawn out, but the relations of its several parts we see go on ad infinitum. They cannot change. One asks, are all the oaks that ever grew hidden in the first acorn, if there was one ? Yes, just as casts from a bas relief are hidden in the original.

Only the secretions from the whole of me bear the impress of the whole of me, and can develop into a child like me. Nothing less than a cast from the whole bas relief will reproduce the whole. The cast of an arm, a head, a foot, will not give the whole. The law is unalterable, the result inevitable. But changes may come, new conditions be added. I may throw a thread across the face of the bas relief before taking one cast, and its impress will be handed down by every cast from that cast. This accounts for the transmission of new characteristics in beings—development.

So, of mental or moral, as of physical characteristics. The secretion drawn from the whole of me will bear the impress of the whole of me, my moral as well as physical characteristics. The secretion from part of a human being will not make a human being. It requires the secretion from the whole of me, bearing the impress of the whole of me, to make a child like me. And just as it will have an arm like mine, so it will bear the impress of my mental and moral characteristics. As I form the star in the glass, so I can form " I love you," in candy. Draw out either while ductile to a thread. In one, I will always still find the star, in the other " I love you." Now if we doubled the thread upon itself and catch it in the middle, and, twisting it, draw it out in one thread, that one thread will be doubly marked, containing two stars, or two

" I love you's—which its section will show—or other threads containing other devices may be added and new combinations be added ad infinitum, but the original device, the star or what not, will always be there. Every time it is doubled upon itself, or receives some addition, the thread becomes more complex. In a certain sense more " highly organized."

Like begets like. The complicated begets not the simple, but the complicated; and let any accident add a further complication and a further complication is begotten, to be handed down to the future. The cast from the face will be like the face, and the cast from the thread will be like the thread; and the cast from both (the face with the thread across it) will be like both. Every accident adds complexity—this is development. Others have proclaimed development, but I have herein explained it. Others have claimed that it is. I have stated what it is; have shown the mechanical action accounting for it; have shown that it cannot but be. Each time the thread of Venetian glass, by accident or design, doubles on itself, or combines with other threads, the resultant thread contains them all. So with every accident of life, of existence, or design of the creator, adding new shapes, new forms, new qualities to the organism, or the republic of organisms, the secretion bearing the impress of the whole shows these additions. More complicated types must ever arise.

And, as I can chisel the nose off the face in any of the casts, and the cast from that cast lack noses, so any part may be destroyed and disappear. This must not be mistaken for a return to simplicity. It is a further complication. That action of the chisel is an added element in the future.

Nov. 1875.   D. N. R.

THE VENETIAN GLASS VASE.

This is the vase of crystal made in Murano's islet :
Marked I these threads of ruby coursing its stem transparent,
Marked them and read there its structure, the law of its being, mine also,
The law of its race, of all races, the relation of atoms unchanging ;
Saw how the egg and the wheat seed secrete from the whole of its forebear,
Bears all its impress, must grow in its likeness ;
Revealed, saw there haply a secret hid to men's senses forever.

The sacerdote says, "Let me tell you what is discreet; let me have the sole say of what is 'done in the fear of God,' in 'reverence.'

And I will say, "the fear of God" has nothing to do with this earth or the laws of creation; or, as men say, the methods of nature, its methods of construction and destruction. Leave all this as unworthy of your attention, as made to ensnare you, as the work of the devil. Consider both construction and destruction as only bewilderment. That sounds a little unreasonable; but reason, too, is a snare. Trust us. We have discarded reason, and do not walk by sight. Let us lead. Leave everything to us. That will make life dull? O, no, dear child, we will let you have plenty of amusements, childish amusements fitted for you, dear child, "distractions." Riches? Accumulate them and we will give you our blessing, help you to hold them, and help you to enjoy them. Love? Well, this is a delicate subject, not to be plainly spoken of. In theory you and all men must have purity complete, that is absolute continence, except in monogamous marriage.

But, of course, this is for many impossible. That that must be which is impossible; that duty, according to revelation (according to us,) requires what creation, according to common experience denies—is a little puzzling to the mind, and is an instance of why we don't want you to use your minds —and prefer your leaving thinking and reason to us. Acknowledge our right by miraculous appointment, our divine right (like the divine right of kings, which was once, when our teaching on that subject was listened to, as well as our teaching on other subjects, that are still listened to, such a

pens than is known.) And so they have to come to us to get
the bruised particles somewhat cemented together with a little
of our different patent sacerdotal cements: all patents, all mon-
oplies Yes, they have to come to us. They have to come to
us or be damned—at least we tell them so—and we take care
to tell them so in infancy and earli-st childhood when impres-
sions are easiest made and made strong and ineffacable. Once
get a child thoroughly frightened and he never recovers from
it. He remains a child, a trembling, timid child, cowering in
the secret recesses of his consciousness as long as he has consciousness. He never out-grows it. He never develops that
part of him into a man. He is ours—our slave, or as we
say, our "child" forever.

Well, so you see the Creator works for us after ; ll. He has
his ways, and we have our ways. They are different ways. and
we find our account in it. It all works nicely for our interest
—for our little game. We can piously say, "all things work
together for good," and add (if you understand by the phrase
ourselves, about which doubts will occasionally obtrude themselves, but not often, we are too busy for that,) "for them
that love God." O, we can quote Scripture—the highest and
noblest Scripture—as well as the Devil, for our purpose, for
our interested purpose, our men-roping-in purpose, and our
self-deceiving purpose. Yes, we use Scripture "for the terror
of them that do evil (or, at least, do what is against our interest which is as much as we can generally attend to,) and the
praise of them that do well," (or, at least, for our interest.)

Now, dear child, son, understand our position. I may have
been a little indiscreetly confidential or diffusive. I may have
forgotten you a bit, and may have been thinking aloud. But
you will soon forget it. While you will not forget what we
took good care to impress upon your callow sensorium in infancy, viz: There is a hell of unutterable horror, and you will
go there unless you do as we say. And you can't do as we say.
So you are bound to go there unless we get you out of your
scrape. Well, then, dear child, it is simple; amuse yourself if

worldly wise; or don't amuse yourself if a dreamer of an ideal perfection, and so given to magnify slips of momentary thought or wish, or hope, or wonder, (for wondering about things leads to speculation, to thought, which we disapprove of. We, and we only must do the thinking for men, and we will discuss as to what is for cur interest, as we have done from time to time in councils, and will put forth what is to be held—not thought about, that is our business.) So amuse yourselves. Have a good time, or deny yourselves and have a bad time. But either way, be sure to come to us at last for your hell-escape-ticket and you will be all right. Pay our price. It is regulated like the bills of our professional brethren, the body doctors. Once the same men practiced both callings—body curing and soul curing (or body-killing and soul-killing—ha! ha! but I am really indiscreet.) Our prices are regulated by what we think a man will stand. The more afraid of hell you are the more is the favor to you of getting you out of that fear; and so the more you must pay for your hell-escape-ticket. Now, dear child, kneel down and make your submission. There; God bless you. *Au revoir.*"

But would it not be well if you and I whether sacerdotes like the above, or other, or whatever we are, should kneel down and pray: *not our way, O Lord, but the best way.*

We seem to be here, *i.e.*, to be conscious, and so conscious of being, conscious and conscious of our surroundings. We seem to have joy and pain, or comfort and discomfort, rest, or, at any rate, unrest, fatigue, weariness and desire of rest; we seem to have the pain of hunger, and, at certain ages and times, of desire. If this hunger or desire have promise of assuagement they themselves give pleasure; we call them "good appetite," "le tendre desir," etc; and if that prospect is absent, they are torture. Tantalus is tortured with a quenchless thirst, a hunger for fluids, and so on. Yet, "If I had a good foaming beaker of cool ale here," cries the man in the hot railway flying train, "I would give twenty-five dollars for this thirst."

We seem to learn to profit by our experiences of comfort, or at least of discomfort, assuaging thirst, satisfying hunger, gratifying desire, getting warm when suffering from cold, or finding shelter from storms, etc.

When thirsty we learn to go where we expect to find drink; when hungry, food, etc. The distance we go seems to depend on previous experiences (our own or, as is now suggested, those too of our ancestors). The babe turns its lips to seek its mother's breast. The stag goes leagues through the forest to find the salt licks. So seeking, we show ourselves, so to speak, idealists, conceiving an ideal, an ideal of good, in the sensorium; and then, like idealists, seeking to get a practical, a material, a real, realization of such ideal.

In our surroundings, our "here," we seem to become ware of the existence of other beings. We are more or less able to communicate with them, either by our, or their, "mute indirections" (*i.e.*, by watching them and judging of them and their wishes and intentions by their conduct as far as we see and note it. Thus the beasts seem to communicate to each other much intelligence as to the whereabouts of food, shelter, etc., and especially when they are in trouble and need help); or, we seem to be able to communicate by articulate speech, whose forms, languages, differ, and have to be, because arbitrary, learned more or less laboriously.

By speech, inarticulate or articulate, other beings seem to tell us of their experience.

We seem, some of us, able to go farther and not only to tell our experience, that others may profit by it in parallel cases, and able, combined with others, to pass it from mouth to mouth, so that it may reach those far distant from the first speaker, far distant in space and unseen, and even, (by the old telling it to the young, who, retaining it in their memories, can tell it again to those younger than themselves, and so, the process being repeated for generations) to those far distant in time also;—we seem, I say, some of us, able not only to do this, through a chain of individuals, but further able, some one or more individuals, to make a record, a mark, a totem, make a trail which can be known and read of another, if taught; and so, by means of such marks or trails, to convey information without personal contact, to convey information, as we say, "by letter." And farther we seem to have an elaborate system of such marks, so that very abstruse and remote and delicate discriminations of ideas may all thus be conveyed from one to another, from one to many, from one moment of time to a period of time far distant. These communications if found useful, if found to convey valuable knowledge learned by experience of others far distant in time or space we shall naturally, as in the case of our own more dearly bought experience, highly value. Such records will amount to rules, formula, for getting what we want in certain cases, or avoiding evils in other certain cases.

And, if such rules are adopted generally by all our tribe, by all our fellows, by all around us similarly situated to ourselves, they will form, practically, a law, or body, or series, of laws. We shall at least be held responsible and subject to reproach from our fellows if evil come to us or them through our failure to follow such rules, to be guided by such laws. No wonder, then, that respect for Laws will be great, and will be strongly inculcated by those who most appreciate their value, by those of most experience, the old, and no wonder that the faithful exact observance of laws will, by those experienced be inculcated on the inexperienced, the young.

It will not surprise us then if, in order to impress upon the young, the importance of observance of tribal laws and the like, the old stretch a point of morals, and, feeling that the end justifies the means, threaten the young not only with penalties that experience has shown come from neglect of keeping the law, but farther with penalties imposed by the tribe or within the tribe (the fear of the certainty of which will restrain the weak ones in the tribe) and pen-

alties (which will restrain even the strong ones of the tribe) which have no other existence than in their imagination,—the imagination of the speaker or that of some other old fellow who has passed such product of his imagination on, for use, to his pals. We are not surprised to find laws therefore inculcated not only by declaring and showing their value, but also inculcated by threats of imaginary disaster in case of violation. And again, as such threats would soon get often found out as vain and so be laughed at, if they partook of the nature of an immediate visible—say bodily—harm—which, when it did not follow, and in the cases where it did not follow, would disprove the likelihood of its following in other like cases—we are not surprised that remote harms, invisible, perhaps not bodily or material at all, should have great vogue as threats. In proportion as the truth of such threats could not be disproved, they would be feared and more or less believed in, and so would be effective. It is no wonder, then, that superstition grows, and has played a great part in the world ; has done so, and will do so, changing its forms, perhaps, but ever in the field. And again, as the joy of threatening and causing fear, and the joy of compelling by fear folk to do what otherwise they don't want to do, is an ecstatic joy, it is not surprising that old men and old women and some younger ones give themselves this ecstatic delight—and don't stint themselves in it. Nor again are we surprised that the beneficiaries of the system combine, and support one another in their assertions, and that—the Church is born.

The old Hebrews, for example, fearing hunger and neglect when their strength is failing teach that they hold a power to curse or bless, bring good or evil on others now and in the years to come. The blessing of Abraham, Isaac, and Jacob, was thus looked upon as something mechanical, a something to be got, as by Jacob, even by trickery and fraud ; and so on.

Now, meddling in other folk's affairs, interfering, controlling (delicious thought) is not only one of the most delightful—in some ways the most delightful of human—and as we sometimes see with shepherd's dogs, canine—joys—united doubtless with virtue, both in dogs and men, upited to, but not entirely, virtue ;—flattery of the egotism going for a great part in any case probably,—not only is this one of the most delightful joys, but it is one the appetite for which grows by what it feeds on in the most inordinate way. Nero, of old, and the poor modern emperor of a vast European country, occu-

pied, not with what will make people happy, but what will, in the one case minister say to his pleasure, or in the other case to his sense of " what he owes to the memory of his father " (it would be fine—if it wasn't ridiculous,) are instances, and pitiful instances, of this feature—I had almost said this disease—the lust of power.*

But it is only when the Church, the medicine man organized, takes a hand at interference that the completest misery ensues ; completest misery ensuing on completest interference. And when we reflect that this complete interference can never be had until the majority are convinced (the majority in numbers or power) of its importance, its, so to speak, divine mission, convinced by teaching, or by force and the sense of their own helplessness, we begin to get some idea of the difficulty, the almost hopelessness, of reform in Church or State ; or, at least, in either so long as either one stands by the other. However cruel the absolutism of the King, reform is difficult if the Church teaches that the King can do no wrong. However cruel the persecutions by the Church, their reform is difficult if the King upholds the Church in its cruelty. We are not surprised, then, to find, in what seems to be the history of the less distant past, of which alone as yet we seem to have much of a history, we are nor surprised I say to find long stretches of suffering more or less impatiently, and yet patiently, borne. And again, if laws and customs, whether established for the convenience of rulers, or the profit of certain classes, or the convenience of society at large, are declared by the Church to be of divine origin, and their violation certain to be followed by dire penalties, not only those imposed by the civil authority, but penalties certain to be sent of Heaven, on the violators, then little is there likelihood, while belief in the utterances of the Church remains, for any change in those laws. And if the Church profits by the violations of those laws, profits by the sale of pardons for such violations, what likelihood is there that the Church will advocate any change in such laws? Fortunately it seems that the Church is powerless without the aid of the State. It seems so ; for the Church seems ever changing with the changing

---

* The pose of strut and swell and brag of another of the most prominent monarchs of the present day, and the "me big injun " brag of himself and his officers and army and supporters is one of the most notable—and disgusting—instances of this foolish weakness ; indicative perhaps in this case of what is only possible among an imperfectly civilized people or social phase in whatever country admired and accepted.

fortune of kings. And when the King is the People at Large? Then, it seems as if, first that branch of the Church that least profited by the retaining of the old laws, and then, little by little, other branches, would rearrange their views of what laws are divinely commissioned, until, at last, the branch that elects to change least or not to change at all, will dwindle, be lost, forgot, as one swamped — as the Egyptian Church (which taught there was no salvation without embalmment of a man's dead body by the Church's priests) slowly expired, dwindled away, was swamped and died, and was lost at last, beneath the new views following upon, first the Greek, then the Roman, then the early Christian, and almost or quite up to the Arab and Mahometan, domination.

In all these Churches, hitherto, men's habit of thought, bolstered some by the interests of priests, has held a notion that a thwarting of the instincts of nature was a great virtue; its successful thwarting or fencing in was "purity," the opposite was "impurity." Virtue it was, doubtless, in many, if not in all cases. That is always virtue that brings blessing, or most blessing; always unvirtue that brings only or any needless pain and harm to self or others. But purity or impurity it was only in a strained sense, founded on a denial of nature and a belief that man was *wrongly made*. It is as if we were angry and ashamed that a repeating watch struck the hours, and called it unvirtuous and "impure" therefor; and made various hindrances to its so striking, or at least only regarded its striking as not unvirtue if done within certain prescribed limits which we set down. We can readily see that if our prescribed limits tallied exactly with the limits fixed for its striking by the constructor, or construction, of the watch, all would be well. No harm would be done by our interference, our rules, our laws, for its striking; no harm or good. It would be wholly as if we had made no laws, and our action would be harmless because in effect inoperative. But if we did otherwise, and tried to set bounds other than those provided for by the construction of the watch, we should be likely either to injure the watch by our meddling with it and preventing its striking as intended, or else we should be likely to injure our tempers by becoming wroth if the watch struck when we said it ought not to. It is precisely these two things which happen as a result of laws and notions about purity and impurity imposed arbitrarily, with good intentions or otherwise, by State or Church, and by society at large and its utterances, its literature, plays, poems,

romances, histories, treatises, philosophy, morals, ethics, et id
omne genus. In so far as they start with the unanalyzed conven-
tional notion of what is "impurity," "the pure," etc., they do harm,
if their idea is one not exactly in accordance with the construction
—the physical construction—of man. They may do good by their
laws, even if they defend them on false grounds. But, at the same
time, they are likely to do harm by defending them on false grounds,
whether the action of the laws themselves ever result in harm or
not. Falsehood is a miserable thing and not the less miserable when
put forth by the Church, or the State, or society, or the literary artist or workman. Indeed it is the more hurtful in proportion as its
utterer professes a regard for truth. It was this that made the
French recognize the distinction between the inconvenient and the
wrong, the sinful, the impure. We may avoid things and insist on
others avoiding them where they will bring harm on them or theirs,
or on us or ours, or on any one; but that does not justify us in doing
so on false grounds, on calling things by false names, or *befogging
the moral sense* of anybody even the most simple.

We seem to think nearly everybody most simple except ourselves; and thus to justify ourselves in giving them untrue reasons
for conduct; either thinking thereby to save their innocence, and
ignorance, their "purity;" or we give them guesses, or untrue reasons, as truth, merely because we are too stupid or too lazy or too
ignorant ourselves to be able to tell them facts or true reasons, and
too anxious to retain their respect for our supposed infallibility and
all-knowingness to frankly acknowledge that we don't really understand the matter ourselves, or, at any rate, think it would be better
for them if they did not try to learn more about it.

We seem, poor human race, to be compassed about with lies from
the first, from the infancy of the race and from the infancy of each
one of us.

I suppose of all sins the greatest sin, of all ignoblenesses the
most ignoble, of all unworthinesses the most unworthy, is to inflict
loss on others (say to secure aggrandizement to ourselves,) by an appeal, a crafty or ungenerous appeal, to others' nobility. This, and
not having courage to say we don't know, and inventing mendacious
explanations and, alas, mendacious threats, seem to explain fully
enough,—along with the mystification from using the same word in
several meanings, and along with assuming that what touches our
emotions ought to convince us,—explains I say fully enough the

cause of a great, perhaps the greater, part of the past misery of the human race.

We seem, if we reflect on this long enough, to see in the recognition of this (the recognition of the wrongs that using the deceiving methods just cited must lead to) as it were a round of a ladder on which we stand at last; while up and beyond us stretch rounds on which we have yet no secure footing, rounds ungrasped perhaps, but more or less clearly seen, the ideals of men, the ideals of the men of our day, and with them, the ideals of those to come after us even, which we cannot individualize but yet can see as a vanishing series, mounting to the skies, lost in light, in ineffable beauty and blessing; and, with them also, the ideals of the men of the past, the remoter past, the far far distant, the remotest past; ideals that are still ideals, still unrealized, and so beyond us, among the rounds, round on round, above and beyond us. And then we seem to be aware of how lately some of the rounds up which we have stepped in our short individual lives perhaps, or rounds up which our race has perhaps slowly and laboriously clambered, have each in turn been vague ideals; ideals often seemingly almost hopeless of ever being reached (as when men in America not so long ago dreamed of, but as almost hopeless, the abolishing of American negro slavery). And, clinging where we stand, a solemn sense comes over us. So far hath the Lord helped us? In the unknown all is, for us, as dark; in the known all uncertain; we scarcely dare to say more than that we seem to be here. Are we to falter? Climb no more? Look no more upward? Close our eyes? Or can we do so, even if we would!

LETTERS.

" While endless ages wax and wane."

To the fair flow'ret of the sun 'tis given
To be immortal in the seeds it bears,
Fall they but haply where the ground is ripe
That, as if loving, gently nurtures them
    To breeding. And so, on and on ;
Each flower's new seeding taking chance the same.

But unto men, high gifted, flower of ages past,
    Bred in the sun and nurtured on and on,
An immortality is given in record made,
    (Yet to the sun flower too, in vanish'd forms)
    Long buried, brought to light long ages on ;
Records quick read of coming men to follow on,
Fixing the sequences that breed a borrow'd thought ;
    And, as the sequence of recorded notes
    Of vanish'd song wake still again
Old echoes in new hearts, so on and on ;
Haply to be while endless ages wax and wane.